NO MORE BUTTERFLIES

Overcoming Stagefright, Shyness, Interview Anxiety, & Fear of Public Speaking

Peter Desberg, Ph.D.

New Harbinger Publications

Publisher's Note

This publication is designed to provide accurate and authoritative information in regard to the subject matter covered. It is sold with the understanding that the publisher is not engaged in rendering psychological, financial, legal, or other professional services. If expert assistance or counseling is needed, the services of a competent professional should be sought.

To Cheryll

CONTENTS

PREFACE

The Treatment of the "Butterflies" in a Nutshell

Woody Allen said, "Any theory that you can put in a nutshell deserves to be in one." Well, here is why people get stagefright, and how to control it—in a nutshell.

The Cause

Everyone likes to look good in front of an audience. If you think they will evaluate you negatively, you will become anxious and experience tension and fear. It will be even worse if the consequences of that negative evaluation are serious.

The Cure

In this book you will learn that it is your thoughts and predictions that actually cause the fear you experience when you are speaking to an audience. When these predictions are accurate, you will learn to take necessary preventive steps, and when your predictions are inaccurate, you will learn to rethink them.

That is the big picture. Now I can begin to chop it up a bit. In this book I will be showing you techniques that attack your beliefs about stagefright at several levels, giving you the means to learn to control it. You will learn to deal with your fear on three different levels:

1. Emotions: You will learn physical and mental relaxation techniques to help reduce feelings of panic and discomfort when you perform.

2. Thoughts: You will learn the relationship between how you think and why you experience butterflies. You will learn techniques to rethink some long-held beliefs that you may not even be aware of.

3. Actions: You will learn many techniques that will make it easier to perform in front of audiences. This will have a twofold effect:

- You will have increased skills in performing.

- Your increased skills will affect how you *think* about performing, and those new thoughts will help reduce your stagefright.

As you go through the book and complete the exercises designed to teach you to control your fear of performing before others, you can begin to enjoy some of the rewards of successfully presenting yourself to an audience. Whether you are being interviewed by a single person or speaking before a thousand people you will join the many people I have worked with who have reported increased success and self-confidence.

How To Use This Book

This book is based on a proven method developed and tested on many people going through my Stagefright Workshops, individual clients, and university students. Going through this book will not be a passive experience for you. You will be asked to interact with the book in designing and carrying out your own improvement program.

There is a difference between *listening* and *learning*. *Reading* is like listening, but worse because you cannot even ask questions. Listening and reading are *passive* processes, while learning is *active*. Think of learning situations in which you have been active or passive. For example, you may have been a passenger being driven to someone's house several times, but the first time you try to drive there yourself, you often cannot remember where it is. Then, after the first time that you have to actually drive there, you can always find it again. The difference is that driving yourself is an active learning process, while being driven is passive.

In this book I have attempted to go a bit further than most self-help books. Rather than tell you about how others have learned to control stagefright, you will be coached through actually learning to control it yourself. To this end, this book is written more as a procedures manual than a self-help book. Instead of just telling you the major principles involved in controlling the butterflies, and giving you a series of related clinical anecdotes, the book is interactive. You will be asked to take specific diagnostic inventories and perform specific exercises.

How the Book Is Organized

1. Each chapter contains explanations, case studies, and exercises so that you can learn to control your stagefright by precept, example, and experience.

2. Wherever possible, chapters are built around the actual tasks and exercises you will be performing.

3. *All* parts of the concept are explained so you will have a fuller understanding of it. For example, I will talk about a concept's emotional and psychological aspects so you can understand *why* it has the effects it does, and why certain things you do will help overcome your fear.

4. I guide you in choosing the techniques and treatments that are most appropriate for you.

What You Will Have To Do

To get as much as possible from this book, you will have to:

1. Get some paper and a pencil (or pen if you have a lot of confidence). You will be learning to tap into and record your own thoughts. Then you will design your own treatment.

2. Do a lot of *thinking* and *imagining* about what it is like for you to perform before an audience. You will discover that it is actually this *thinking* and *imagining* you do that causes most of your stagefright.

3. Do a series of exercises. Before we go any further, you should understand that these exercises have been designed to be *minimally*

discomforting. Obviously, stagefright is an area surrounded by a great deal of tension and it's not possible to learn to control it without getting a little uneasy. To this end, I have designed these exercises to be as easy and non-threatening as possible. Everything will be done gradually, as *you* feel you are prepared. You will be making your own judgments about how fast you would like to go. The rewards you will get for letting people see who you really are and performing successfully in front of them will more than compensate for any tension you experience along the way.

This book is based on years of experimental and clinical work. I have tried every technique, exercise, and activity in this book with groups in my workshops, and individuals in therapy. For anything to be included in this book, it had to pass the most demanding test of all—*it had to work!*

THE BEGINNING

Before you read another word, turn the page and take the *D-M Stage-fright Inventory*. It is a simple way for you to see how much stagefright you currently have, and it will give you a basis to evaluate your progress at the end of the book.

D-M STAGEFRIGHT INVENTORY

Directions: Each item of this inventory is composed of a group of statements. Select the one that *best* describes the way you react when you perform before an audience. Circle the *number* beside the statement you select.

A

0 I do not try to avoid situations in which I must perform.
1 I occasionally try to avoid situations in which I must perform.
2 I usually try to avoid situations in which I must perform.
3 I always try to avoid situations in which I must perform.

B

0 I am not afraid that I will forget or blank out when performing.
1 I am sometimes afraid that I will forget or blank out on part of my performance.
2 I am afraid I will forget or blank out on large parts of my performance.
3 I am afraid that I will forget or blank out totally when performing.

C

0 I do not think others will be bored when I am performing.

1 I sometimes think others will be bored when I am performing.

2 I often think others will be bored when I am performing.

3 I always think others will be bored when I am performing.

D

0 When I perform, I do not experience difficulty in breathing.

1 When I perform, I sometimes experience difficulty in breathing.

2 When I perform, I often experience difficulty in breathing.

3 When I perform, I always experience difficulty in breathing.

E

0 I do not get nervous performing for an audience who is as competent or less competent than I.

1 I occasionally get nervous performing for an audience who is as competent or less competent than I.

2 I usually get nervous performing for an audience who is as competent or less competent than I.

3 I always get nervous performing for an audience who is as competent or less competent than I.

F

0 I do not think others will ridicule my performance.

1 I sometimes think others will ridicule my performance.

2 I often think others will ridicule my performance.

3 I always think others will ridicule my performance.

G

0 I am unaffected by the consequences of my performance.

1 I get nervous only when the consequences of my performance are very important.

2 I get nervous when the consequences of my performance are moderately important.

3 I get nervous regardless of the consequences.

H

0 I do not think that I will perform poorly.

1 I sometimes think that I will perform poorly.

2 I often think that I will perform poorly.

3 I always think that I will perform poorly.

I

0 I do not think that others will dislike me when I perform.

1 I sometimes think that others will dislike me when I perform.

2 I often think that others will dislike me when I perform.

3 I always think that others will dislike me when I perform.

J

0 I am not affected by the size of the audience.

1 I only get nervous performing for a very large audience.

2 I get nervous performing for small audiences.

3 All audiences make me nervous.

K

0 I never have difficulty in concentrating when performing.

1 I sometimes have difficulty in concentrating when performing.

2 I often have difficulty in concentrating when performing.

3 I always have difficulty in concentrating when performing.

L

0 People do not feel sorry for me when they see me perform.

1 People sometimes feel sorry for me when they see me perform.

2 People often feel sorry for me when they see me perform.

3 People always feel sorry for me when they see me perform.

M

0 I do not feel nervous when performing for strangers.

1 I occasionally feel nervous when performing for strangers.

2 I usually feel nervous when performing for strangers.

3 I always feel nervous when performing for strangers.

N

0 The audience does not sense that I do not know my material.

1 The audience sometimes senses that I do not know my material.

2 The audience often senses that I do not know my material.

3 The audience always senses that I do not know my material.

O

0 I do not think that there is something about me that audiences dislike.

1 I occasionally think that there is something about me that audiences dislike.

2 I often think that there is something about me that audiences dislike.

3 I always think that there is something about me that audiences dislike.

P

0 I do not get embarrassed when performing.

1 I sometimes get embarrassed when performing.

2 I often get embarrassed when performing.

3 I always get embarrassed when performing.

Q

0 I am usually well organized when performing.

1 I sometimes appear disorganized when performing.

2 I often appear disorganized when performing.

3 I always appear disorganized when performing.

R

0 I do not expect to be put on the spot and attacked.

1 I sometimes expect to be put on the spot and attacked.

2 I often expect to be put on the spot and attacked.

3 I always expect to be put on the spot and attacked.

S

0 When performing in public, I do not experience trembling or shaking.

1 When performing in public, I sometimes experience trembling or shaking.

2 When performing in public, I often experience trembling or shaking.

3 When performing in public, I always experience trembling or shaking.

T

0 When I perform, I am usually well rehearsed.

1 When I perform, I sometimes do not rehearse enough.

2 When I perform, I often do not rehearse enough.

3 When I perform, I never rehearse enough.

U

0 If I perform well, the audience will not find anything wrong.

1 If I perform well, the audience occasionally still finds something wrong.

2 If I perform well, the audience often still finds something wrong.

3 If I perform well, the audience always finds something wrong.

V

0 I do not feel anxious once I have gotten started with my performance.

1 I feel somewhat anxious after I have gotten started with my performance.

2 I feel very anxious after I have gotten started with my performance.

3 I feel extremely anxious after I have gotten started with my performance.

W

0 I do not expect to make a lot of mistakes.

1 I sometimes expect to make a lot of mistakes.

2 I often expect to make a lot of mistakes.

3 I always expect to make a lot of mistakes.

X

0 I do not expect the audience to reject my point of view.

1 I sometimes expect the audience to reject my point of view.

2 I often expect the audience to reject my point of view.

3 I always expect the audience to reject my point of view.

Y

0 I do not feel nervous when performing for people who do not know me.

1 I sometimes feel nervous when performing for people who do not know me.

2 1 often feel nervous when performing for people who do not know me.

3 1 always feel nervous when performing for people who do not know me.

Scoring the Inventory

Add up the total number of points you have circled. Use the scale below to interpret your current level of stagefright on the inventory:

Above 40 .... Very High Stagefright

30-39 .... High Stagefright

20-29 .... Moderate Stagefright

0-19 .... Low Stagefright

0-9 .... Minimal Stagefright

1

EXPLAINING THE BUTTERFLIES

The Case of Barbara G.

Barbara G. was a middle manager in a pharmaceutical company. She had been in the same position for the past four years and had been watching several younger coworkers rise through the company at a faster rate than she. At this moment she is waiting for her name to be announced as the next speaker in a promotional talk for a new product. Even though she is a competent chemist, she has always been uncomfortable speaking in front of large groups of people.

> I can't believe that they all showed up, even the district manager . . . Look at them out there . . . I hope I don't sound like a complete jerk! God, my temples are throbbing. . . I can't catch my breath . . . Why don't they just call me instead of going through all these announcements and introductions . . . Maybe it won't be so bad this time . . . and I won't forget all the . . .

As Barbara heard her name introduced, a wave of panic overtook her. She tried to rehearse her opening joke, but it seemed to make no sense to her, so she discarded it. Afraid that she would forget her main, opening points, she tried to go over them in detail. Unfortunately, all she could think about was her disastrous talk at last year's promo meeting.

> I've got to focus on the first three points. They're the key to
> my talk. . . . Oh God, there's Wiggins . . . he's been
> salivating over my job. . . . He looks so smug. . . . I can
> barely walk. . . . Please don't let me forget the opening . . . .

Barbara began her talk appearing outwardly calm, although inside she was trembling. As she was presenting the three basic ideas of her speech, she noticed that she was already talking about the third idea, but had never mentioned the second. Her mind sped forward, trying to think about the implication of the changed order, and she got tripped up trying to go back to the second idea.

> Oh no, I sound like I don't know what the hell I'm talking
> about. . . . What can I do to get them back? Wiggins is
> smirking. . . . Look at my hands shaking. . . . Is that snake
> whispering something to the District Manager? Throat
> feels so tight . . . got to calm down! God, are the two of
> them laughing? I can hardly breathe. . . . It looks like
> Wiggins just got my promotion. . . .

Barbara G. has stagefright! Stagefright is the fear of having your performance evaluated negatively. In the *Book of Lists*, Amy Wallace, David Wallechinsky, and Irving Wallace rank fear of public speaking as the *number one phobia in America*. Fear of dying is number six! In a recent national poll, over 40 percent of the people sampled said that they were afraid of public speaking.

It is not necessary to have a large audience for this fear to occur. Often the audience is composed of a single person. Some other common examples of stagefright are going on a job interview, asking someone for a date, performing sports in front of spectators, making an important business call, and asking the boss for a raise.

Anyone can experience the butterflies, not just shy or insecure people.

Here is a brief description of what you go through as you are actually performing and experiencing stagefright:

1. You make a prediction that there is something threatening or dangerous in the performance situation that can lead to failure. You make predictions about *every* situation you're about to enter. You may predict that you will have a good time at a party or a bad meeting with your boss. As you are about to perform anything in front of an audience, you may imagine a number of things that might go wrong. You may worry about forgetting something, appearing disorganized, or being boring. Ask anyone who has spoken in front of an audience—*the list of potential problems to worry about is quite long*. These fear-provoking thoughts come from many sources, including your own past failures, observing other people in similar situations, or simply having an active imagination.

Although Barbara G. was not a particularly anxious or insecure person, she believed that she was not a good public speaker. She thought that she was likely to forget key elements in her talk. These predictions would be enough to frighten anyone. She believed that these predictions were reasonable because she had a bad experience in a similar situation a year before. In addition, she predicted how bad the consequences of a poor performance would be for her—not getting a promotion.

2. You experience anxiety as a result of your fear-provoking thoughts. Feelings and emotions are produced by thoughts! If you believe you will go in front of an audience and have difficulty, you *will* become frightened. You may not even be aware that you have made any predictions about the event, but these predictions end up determining how you will feel *before* and *during* that performance.

Because Barbara G. predicted she would do badly in her talk, she scared herself. She experienced many of the common physical symptoms of anxiety: fast heart rate, shortness of breath, weakness in her legs, shaking hands, tight throat, and so on.

3. You use the anxiety and discomfort you feel as evidence confirming the accuracy of your original prediction. Once you have predicted that a situation will turn out badly, you begin to look for evidence to support that prediction. As you continually inspect yourself and your audience for signs that things are going badly, it is easy to make this come about. You use the first jolt of adrenaline that accompanies anxiety as very strong evidence that your fear is well-founded. It is *proof* that things are really as bad as you feared . . . or worse.

When Barbara G. first felt those intense physical symptoms, she realized that she was anxious. The combination of her symptoms and her realization *proved* just how bad things really were. *She was afraid of being afraid*. Her level of anxiety rose as she felt the first physical signs of anxiety.

4. You make new predictions about what will happen using both the original fear-provoking thoughts and the confirming anxiety they caused as a basis for more intense negative predictions. Making predictions is a *continuing* action. You do not just make a single prediction and then the process is over. You will use *any* new piece of information as a basis for updating your present prediction. As your original prediction is confirmed with anxiety, it becomes the basis for the next prediction. Moreover, this new prediction is regarded as more serious because it is based on *actual data*.

Based on the anxiety that Barbara G. was experiencing, she revised her prediction—downward! She took this new prediction more seriously because it was supported by evidence, rather than just being a hunch about what might happen. This caused her to predict that things were going to get worse.

This series of events continues in a vicious cycle, with results ranging from mild discomfort to total performance dysfunction. Each time you get new evidence that confirms a prediction, you make a new prediction which incorporates that evidence, and leads to greater anxiety.

5. Since the brain can only focus attention on one complex mental task at a time, the more you focus on assessing your anxiety, the more the task you are performing will be interfered with and interrupted. Distractions will interfere with the processes of memory and attention. Getting scared in front of an audience presents a *huge* distraction. The more you focus your attention on your current state of anxiety and distress, the less you will be able to concentrate on your performance. This will cause problems for the performance such as memory loss and disorganization.

Barbara G. was definitely working against herself. As she was giving her talk, her attention was split four ways: (1) she was thinking about her talk, (2) she was monitoring the audiences reactions, (3) she was assessing her own state of anxiety, and (4) she was monitoring her own deteriorating performance.

The more Barbara divided her attention, the more she stopped focusing on her talk. Because she let her mind wander off the topic, she got disorganized, and began making mistakes. She reversed the order of her opening points because she was concentrating on how scared she was, rather than on the points themselves.

The Basic Causes of Stagefright

The main cause of stagefright is the *fear of negative evaluation*. According to Mark Leary, the amount of stagefright a person experiences in any situation is controlled by two factors which can be represented in a simple formula:

$$\text{Stagefright} = \frac{\text{Importance of the Consequences of the Performance}}{\text{Prediction of a Successful Performance}}$$

Until now, I have only stressed the bottom half of the formula—predicting the outcome. Equally important are the predicted effects, or the consequences, of a poor performance. *The more harmful and long-lasting the consequences of performing poorly can be, the more stagefright you will experience.*

If you were giving a talk before a large audience, you might feel nervous. If your job depended on its success, you would experience much more stagefright. In our example above, one of the reasons Barbara G. got so nervous during her speech was that she imagined serious consequences resulting from her talk. She saw an important promotion depending on her success.

The major complication in dealing with this formula is that both factors in it are *totally subjective*. Everything depends on how *you* see things. Here are a pair of examples that show, by contrast, how both parts of the formula work together:

The Case of Jud H.: Situation 1

Jud H. moved into a new neighborhood. When his son's teacher heard that he was an aerospace engineer, she asked if he would address her eighth grade science class on the possibilities of space travel.

This was a subject about which he knew a great deal, and enjoyed discussing. The audience (a class of fourteen-year-olds) were not at all threatening to him, and the results of the talk would not affect him in any way. According to the formula, there should have been very little stagefright for Jud in this situation. The consequences of his talk were unimportant to him, and the likelihood of a successful outcome was quite high. He gave the talk with confidence and received spontaneous applause from the class. When he finished the talk the students kept him for another fifteen minutes asking him questions. He thoroughly enjoyed the experience.

The Case of Jud H.: Situation 2

At about the same time Jud H. was asked to give the talk in the eighth grade classroom, he was also asked to give a talk at a local PTA meeting. He was very concerned with making a good impression on his neighbors, and saw this as his "Big Opportunity" to present himself to the community.

He had always felt effective on a one-to-one basis, but had rarely talked in large public settings. The few times he did so in school, he was very nervous, and felt that he was very ineffective. Since that time, he had avoided public speaking situations. He thought that when it came to public speaking, very little had changed since his school days.

According to the formula, Jud H. should have experienced a great deal of anxiety talking before the PTA. The consequences were very important to him, because he felt that his acceptance in the new community depended on his talk. His prediction for the outcome was very negative, based on his previous experience.

Jud actively dreaded giving this talk for two weeks. His wife complained about his irritability for days before the event. He convinced himself that his new neighbors would think he was a "lightweight," unworthy of holding an esteemed place in the community. When Jud finally gave his talk, he experienced feelings of panic, and later said he could barely remember anything he said.

I later pointed out the difference between the two situations to Jud. He discovered that he was not necessarily a "bad public speaker," but rather that there were certain elements in the situation that triggered his anxiety. In my own research, in workshops, and in individual therapy, I have found no relationship between general measures of how secure or insecure people are and how often they experience stagefright.

Stagefright is not a personality trait, either. Some people believe that there are the *haves* and the *have nots*. The haves will get nervous performing in front of *any* audience, and the have nots will *never* experience it. This is simply not true! Stagefright is not a mental disorder or personality trait that you either have or don't have. Everyone feels stagefright at some time or other. It depends on the *situation*. It is very common to find a man who can yell at his wife and children in the morning, and barely be able to say a word to a prospective employer during an important job interview in the afternoon. It is not that people automatically get nervous talking to other people—they get nervous during *particular situations.*

The Mechanics of Stagefright

Anyone who has experienced stagefright recognizes events similar to those Barbara G. went through. Learning to recognize these events is one of the first steps in learning to control it. In an excellent book entitled *Understanding Social Anxiety*, social psychologist Mark Leary points out that there are two main factors that determine how much stagefright you will experience:

1. Your prediction about how well you think you will perform. *The more you predict failure and doom, the more stagefright you will experience.*

2. Your evaluation of the importance of the consequences of performing. *The more important you think the consequences of a performance are, the more stagefright you will experience.*

Practice Exercise 1: Identifying Situational Factors

Remember that the key word in stagefright is *situational.* Anyone can experience it, depending on the situation. There are many myths concerning the conditions under which stagefright will occur. One of the most common is that it will only occur before a large audience, and the larger the audience, the greater the anxiety. Like many myths, this one is often untrue. A large audience makes some people feel energized and try harder, while it might make others feel more tense. It depends on the situation!

There are many situational factors that determine the level of stagefright you will experience. Here are just a few that can greatly influence your performance: the consequences of the performance to you, how well you believe you will perform, who is in the audience, how skilled or knowledgeable your audience is, or the size of the audience.

Using the form below, identify an event where you spoke or performed well, without experiencing intense anxiety and fear (for example, telling a group of friends at work about your vacation). Then try to identify the aspects of that situation that made you feel comfortable and confident. Perhaps they were all your friends and did not pose a threat to you, or maybe you knew more about your trip than they did so there was no chance of anyone contradicting or challenging you.

The reason I ask you to identify situations in which you are comfortable is so that you can see for yourself that you do not have stagefright, as if it were a trait or disease. You can begin to learn that there are different situational factors present when you experience it.

Then do the same for an event where you did experience stagefright; for example, when you asked the boss for a raise. Identify the situational factors you think were responsible for your anxiety, such as the financial consequences or the chance of being criticized for past mistakes.

Situational Factors in Stagefright

Successful Performance	Unsuccessful Performance
1. Event:	1. Event:
2. Situational Factors:	2. Situational Factors:

As you look at your responses to the above exercise, try to figure out some of the following things:

- Around what sort of people are you most fearful?

- What sort of things are you uncomfortable discussing or doing?

- What size groups seem to affect you?

- What do you think about competition?

Here is an example of how one of our clients did this exercise:

Situational Factors in Stagefright

Successful Performance	Unsuccessful Performance
1. Event:	1. Event:
Describing summer trip to Europe with a group of friends at work. When I came back to work after my trip everyone at work was interested in hearing about my trip. They all gathered in the lunchroom, and wanted details.	*Asking my boss for a raise. My boss has a tendency to be excitable and hostile in conflict situations, and I really needed the additional money because I wanted to begin taking classes in an MBA program. When I finally went in to see him, he remained calm and professional the entire time, but I became a nervous wreck. I forgot several of the key reasons that I wanted to present on behalf of my position.*
2. Situational Factors:	2. Situational Factors:
I think that the talk went well for the following reasons:	*I think that the talk went badly for the following reasons:*
• *They were all my friends and were happy that I enjoyed myself.*	• *I felt panicked about what would happen to me if I didn't get the raise.*
• *They were all genuinely interested in what I had to say.*	• *I told myself that if I couldn't make a forceful presentation to my boss, then he would lose respect for me.*
• *I certainly knew more about the trip than they did.*	
• *Nothing bad would have happened to me if I didn't do a good job of telling them about my trip.*	• *He has turned down several other people whom I thought were deserving.*
• *I wasn't worried about forgetting any aspects of the trip.*	

> - *I went in expecting the worst possible outcome.*
> - *I know that I am not good in face-to-face encounters that require hard negotiating.*

You have just taken a first step toward learning to control your fear by identifying some of the things that worry you. In the next chapter you will learn a series of relaxation exercises so you can deal effectively with the discomfort brought about by stagefright.

Special Considerations: Hypnosis and Drugs

Drugs and hypnosis can often be used to get you through a tough performance, but there are two major problems with using them:

1. How you feel about yourself. If you think that you got through a tough situation because of the drug, rather than on your own ability, then you cannot enjoy your own success. You attribute the success to the drug or hypnotist.

2. If you rely on drugs or hypnosis, what can you do if you are about to perform and no one is there to give you a drug or to hypnotize you?

Summary

This chapter presented the basic mechanics of stagefright.

- The major cause of stagefright is the fear of negative evaluation. It is influenced by two factors: (1) how likely you think you are to perform well, and (2) how important the consequences are.

- Stagefright is based on a series of ongoing predictions that keep escalating in a vicious cycle.

- The amount of anxiety and fear you feel depends on various situational factors

2

LEARNING TO RELAX

In this chapter you will learn to use relaxation techniques to help you reduce tension in anxiety-provoking situations, particularly those involving your fear of performing. You will also learn how to cope with being afraid of being afraid.

These two goals both involve *symptom relief*. Symptom relief means reducing your discomfort without doing anything about the actual causes of it. You may be curious about why I would deal with the symptoms before the causes. There are three important reasons for reducing the unpleasant symptoms of stagefright:

1. It makes you feel better! Getting rid of pain and discomfort is worthwhile for its own sake. If these symptoms were not so unpleasant, stagefright would not be such a problem.

2. Symptom relief keeps your fear from escalating. Remember in the previous chapter I discussed how your rising level of anxiety provides evidence that things are getting worse. Once you learn to control your anxiety level, you will be less likely to experience feelings of runaway anxiety and panic.

3. It helps you overcome *avoidance*. As you will see later, one of the main problems in stagefright is avoidance of the actual performance situation. I have devoted an entire chapter to this problem.

Relaxation Training

Herbert Benson, a professor at the Harvard Medical School and author of the 1975 book *The Relaxation Response*, has researched the area of relaxation training and synthesized many methods. Of all the relaxation techniques available, I selected Benson's method because of its simplicity and proven effectiveness.

All forms of relaxation training end up doing the same thing. They reduce the amount of stimulation sent to the brain. This produces slower heart and breath rates, lower oxygen needs, and reduced muscular tension. All of this, taken together, leads to a feeling of well-being and relaxation throughout the body.

There is perhaps a simpler way to explain what happens during relaxation training. The French satirist Voltaire said, "The art of medicine consists in amusing the patient while nature cures the disease." Likewise, your body will relax itself if you can distract yourself from fear-provoking thoughts. During relaxation training, you are kept so busy concentrating on relaxing that you cannot think about your problems.

A note of caution: If you have high blood pressure, diabetes, or any other condition that requires medication, please consult your physician before beginning relaxation training.

The Relaxation Response

Benson's method has four components:

1. A Quiet Environment: Once you have learned how to relax, you will find these techniques useful in any situation. At the beginning, when you are first learning, you must find the right environment. This consists of a place where you will be free from distractions. There should be no background noise or interruptions.

2. A Mental Device: This is anything that will distract you from having fear-provoking thoughts. Benson suggests mentally repeating a single, one-syllable word. While you are focusing your attention on this word, you cannot be having thoughts such as, "What kinds of hostile questions will my audience ask during the next sales meeting?"

Benson's favorite word is one. He suggests that this word be repeated in time with your exhalations, which should be long and slow.

3. Passive Attitude: You do not make relaxation happen—you let it happen to you. Ironically, the harder you work at relaxation, the more difficult it is to relax.

If you find your mind wandering, and you forget to say the word *one*, it is not a problem. Just start saying it again, as soon as you realize that you have stopped. There is no reason to berate yourself.

4. A Comfortable Position: Loosen your belt or any tight fitting clothes. Lie down on a bed or couch, or sit in a comfortable chair. The key here is to have *total body support*. None of the postural muscles should have to be tensed. If you were to let all your muscles loosen, and make your body "dead weight," your body should feel totally supported.

Relaxation skills are no different than any other skills you may acquire—*they must be practiced to be effective*. Fortunately, it feels great to practice them.

Practice Exercise 2:
The Six Steps of the Relaxation Response

Now that you know these four elements, you are ready to actually begin a relaxation exercise:

1. Get into your relaxed position and close your eyes.

2. Begin to concentrate on your breathing, and slow it down. Breathe through your nose, making your exhale longer than your inhale. You will notice a little tension associated with inhaling, and relaxation brought about by your exhaling. Concentrate on making exhaling feel as pleasurable as possible.

3. Pay attention to the position you are in, and feel each part of you being supported by the couch or bed so that you can relax your muscles further.

4. Begin searching your body for any signs of tension. Start at your feet and work your way up the body. As you find any tension, focus your attention on it, and as you exhale, try to relax it away.

5. Keep breathing slowly through your nose, and begin to think or say the word *one* to yourself. Keep doing this for five to ten

minutes. If you get distracted, go back and continue repeating it. After a few sessions you may want to substitute a word that is more conducive to relaxing such as *calm*.

6. When you are ready to end your relaxation training session, open your eyes and sit up slowly. Take one or two more deep, slow breaths.

Notice that you are both relaxed and alert. You may be used to feeling groggy after waking up from a nap, but this is a very different feeling. You have relaxed and at the same time you have increased the amount of oxygen going to your brain, making you more alert. This is one of the main reasons why you will want to practice relaxing just prior to beginning any performance before an audience.

If you have any difficulty in your practicing, here are a couple of additional considerations that may help you:

- Do not practice within two hours of having eaten a big meal. It is always preferable to practice before meals.

- Experiment with various times of day for scheduling your practice sessions. Some people prefer to do it in the morning, before any new upsets have occurred. Many people find that after work, or even during breaks at work, is suitable. Determine what is the most successful time for you.

Being Afraid of Being Afraid

One of the things that frightens people the most is *being afraid*. When you have fear-provoking thoughts, anxiety will typically follow. The problem I will deal with here is that when people notice that they are afraid, *it makes them more afraid*. The anxiety you feel will make you more anxious. As I mentioned in the introduction, people use anxiety to confirm the fact that their fear-provoking thoughts really are accurate predictions and interpretations.

Once when I asked Barbara G. why she was so worried about talking to a group of people, she said, "Look at how scared I got. The situation I was in must have been dangerous, or I wouldn't have gotten so scared." She was *afraid of being afraid*.

There are two important techniques for dealing with being afraid of being afraid: eliminating surprise and using anxiety as a signal.

Practice Exercise 3: Eliminating Surprise

The worst effects of anxiety occur when you are not prepared for it. The best method for dealing with being afraid of being afraid is making use of your own previous experience. Once you know what being afraid is like, and which situations tend to bring it on, *do not be surprised by it!*

Go through the following steps each time you are aware of having fear-provoking thoughts. (Try this out right now, imagining a scene in which you have to perform in front of an audience that will make you nervous.) Write your responses in the spaces below:

1. How is this situation similar to past situations that have brought on anxiety?

   _____

   _____

   _____

2. How are your thoughts similar to fear-producing thoughts you've had before?

   _____

   _____

   _____

3. Predict what your symptoms will be (rapid heartbeat, trembling hands, and so on).

   _____

   _____

   _____

4. On a scale from one to four, indicate how anxious you are now. Let *one* be the lowest level and *four* be the highest.

   _____

   _____

   _____

5. On the same scale from one to four, indicate the highest level of anxiety you expect to reach.

_____

_____

_____

6. As you actually experience anxiety, yawn and tell yourself, "I knew it!"

Being surprised by fear adds to your discomfort. Make your previous fear pay off by using it to eliminate the element of surprise.

Using Anxiety as a Signal

Instead of being surprised by anxiety, use it as a signal that reminds you to employ your relaxation training. It's really quite simple. Every time you feel the symptoms of anxiety, say the word *relaxation* to yourself, and begin practicing the techniques presented at the beginning of this chapter.

At the first sign of anxiety, focus your attention on your breathing and relaxation exercises. Practice this exercise wherever and whenever you encounter anxiety. It is a way to break a harmful old habit, and replace it with a new, more productive one. Here is an example of using anxiety as a cue for relaxation:

The Case of Alice H.

Alice H. was a biology teacher who returned to school to get her Master's Degree. She reported that before a seminar presentation she would be extremely nervous. She would begin thinking about how she might get disorganized and unable to answer questions put to her by her professor. As she noticed how tense she became, she would use that tension as proof that there really was something to worry about. She knew that she was a reasonable person, and would not be afraid if there was not a real threat to her.

During her first session, I gave her relaxation training. She then learned that every time she got scared, she could use her fear as a reminder to use the relaxation techniques she learned. Often people have the skills needed to cope with difficult situations, but they forget to use them when they are under stress. Because Alice hated anxiety, she practiced the relaxation techniques a great deal.

After practicing relaxation methods, Alice reported having given a successful seminar paper where she experienced a minimum of anxiety. She said that as she was about to start her talk she became afraid that her professor would stop her during the presentation and ask a difficult question. She was afraid that she would not be able to answer it and began to panic. As soon as she noticed her heart pounding and her knees shaking, she began to focus her attention on her breathing. She began giving herself the instructions to relax that she had been practicing. Thinking about the instructions kept her from thinking about her professor and enabled her to relax.

Summary

In this chapter I stressed two main skills:

1. Relaxation skills are designed to help you reduce the unpleasant effects of stagefright. After going through this book and learning all the techniques to control your fear of speaking before a group, you should find yourself tense much less often. But there will still be times when anxiety strikes. These relaxation skills will help relieve the unpleasant symptoms that accompany stagefright, giving your audience an opportunity to discover who you are and what you have to say.

2. Most people are afraid of being afraid. They realize that there must be something wrong, or they would not be afraid. I have presented two techniques to help you control this condition: eliminating surprise by making predictions about when anxiety will occur, and using anxiety as a cue for relaxation.

3

IDENTIFYING FEAR-PROVOKING THOUGHTS

In this chapter I will explain the relationship between fear-provoking thoughts and stagefright and show you how to identify the fear-provoking thoughts that lead to your stagefright.

Thoughts and Emotions

People *think* themselves into emotional states. For you to feel anxiety or fear, you must somehow believe that you are in danger. In the case of stagefright, you predict that *something bad is going to happen to you as you perform*. It is this fear-provoking thought that will make you anxious. Along with this thought is a second prediction that *you will be unable to do anything about it*. This thought heightens the anxiety.

People are often unaware of their own predictions, even though they make them about every event in which they participate. Identifying these fear-provoking thoughts is one of the first steps in learning to control stagefright. This is a difficult task because these thoughts can be very elusive. Since they are the key to learning to control your fear, and since they are so difficult to pin down, in this chapter I will present several different methods for identifying them. First, however, I will put things into context by clarifying the relationship between thinking and emotions.

If you told yourself that something awful was about to happen to you, you would get scared. This is a basic cause of stagefright. Your emotional changes are brought about by changes in your thinking. It does not matter whether you are really in danger. What does matter is *whether you believe you are in danger*. Once you believe you are in danger, you will feel anxiety. You will discover throughout this book that there are many times when you *believe* that you are in danger even though you are not. A large part of learning to control stagefright involves learning how to accurately distinguish between situations that are *really* dangerous and safe situations in which you only *believe* there is danger.

The Case of Mary S.

Mary S. was a biology major at a local university. She was in her early forties and had recently returned to school after pursuing a career for about ten years. She presented her problem as math phobia. It first occurred to me that her problem might be stagefright when I asked her to describe a very fearful math experience.

For Mary, one of the worst things possible was to take a math test while her professor was looking over her shoulder as she worked her problems. The professor appeared to be the audience that scared her.

When Mary was asked how she went about studying, she said that her husband helped her. I thought that he probably browbeat her and became increasingly impatient with her. This soon proved not to be the case. I found out that Mary had another case of stagefright with an audience of one—her husband.

Here is her description of her husband, and his method of teaching math to her:

> He's an engineer and loves math. He's very good at
> breaking down complex problems into simple steps, and
> explaining them clearly. He has the patience of a saint, and
> is always encouraging . . . a perfect teacher.

With all this help available at home, why was she not doing better in math? The answer was discovered when I asked her to identify what her thoughts were while her husband was tutoring her. Below are just a few of the thoughts going through her mind as she was trying to understand and follow her husband's teaching:

- He's such a good teacher, and so patient.

- He'd be able to teach anyone ... unless they were really stupid.

- I'm not following what he's saying ... he's going to think I'm an idiot.

- How can an intelligent man like him love an idiot? I'm going to lose my husband.

- If I don't understand my math, I won't be able to pass my physics, math, and chemistry courses, and I'll flunk out of school.

- I'm losing my husband, my education, and my career. I'm going to have to become a waitress again. I'll be a forty-five-year-old divorced waitress.

While Mary was trying to concentrate on learning math, she was constantly being frightened and distracted by these intrusive thoughts. It became almost impossible for her to learn math, even from a clear, patient teacher. It would be very difficult to learn math while your whole life is crumbling before you. These thoughts made it increasingly difficult for Mary to concentrate, which added to her confusion.

As she realized that she was confused and not learning, she became more scared. Adding to her fears were the consequences that not learning would bring about. Mary found herself in a vicious cycle: the more scared she got, the less she could concentrate on her task. The less she could concentrate, the more scared she got, and so on.

Internal Dialogues

Everybody talks to themselves. Sometimes they are aware of it, but more often they are not. A common example of an internal dialogue is what happens when you want to do something that you know is not good for you, but you know you would enjoy it.

Imagine that you wanted to eat a piece of chocolate cake when you were supposed to be dieting. If you tap into your thoughts carefully, you might hear something like, "Tomorrow I'll run three extra miles." Or you might even say, "I only see my mother once every two weeks, and she feels so bad when I don't eat everything she gives me . . . so for her sake, I'll eat it."

You may actually go back and forth between how much fun it will be and why you should not do it until you reach a resolution. Once you learn to pay attention to it, you will notice that you are *talking to yourself* quite a bit. In this chapter you will learn to notice when you are talking to yourself in a performance situation.

Internal dialogues occur side by side with whatever else you are thinking about, and they often go unnoticed. They tend to become more obvious under stressful situations in which it is necessary to concentrate. These thoughts are often *self-evaluative* in nature. A big problem is that people consider these thoughts to be *true*, and rarely test them out. When these thoughts, or interpretations, predict something unpleasant, unpleasant emotional states like stagefright will result.

Occasionally, the fear-provoking thoughts that lead to stagefright are obvious to you. In far more situations, however, they are not. Many thoughts occur below the level of awareness, and are difficult to identify. They occur very quickly because they are so well-practiced. After a while, they become automatic, in much the same way as starting your car or tying your shoes have become automatic.

Learning To Identify Fear-Provoking Thoughts

Since most people's fear-provoking thoughts are so similar, I am able to present many of the most common ones here, but in this chapter I have to go further and teach you to identify your own fear-provoking thoughts.

Two people may be afraid of the same thing, but be afraid of it for different reasons. These different reasons must be treated as two different fears. As mentioned in the first chapter, the common thread that runs through all thoughts related to stagefright is the *fear of negative evaluation*. The key to identifying fear-provoking thoughts is learning to spot a fear of negative evaluation during your own internal dialogues.

The following exercises were taken directly from my workshops. Since identifying fear-provoking thoughts can be a difficult task, I will ease you into it. In the first exercise on identifying fear-provoking thoughts, I present a sample of negative thoughts from four different situations. The exercise is designed to acquaint you with the types of thoughts that lead to performance anxiety.

Practice Exercise 4: Selecting Relevant Fear-Provoking Thoughts

As you read through each of the following four lists of fear-provoking thoughts, place an "x" next to any you have had in this, or similar situations:

1. Public Speaking

Since this is the most common setting for stagefright, I present it first. These statements came from people who were about to speak in front of an audience.

☐   I will probably forget what I'm going to say.

☐   I'm going to appear disorganized.

☐   They're going to see my hands tremble.

☐   Everyone is going to think I'm boring.

☐   A lot of people in the audience know more about this topic than I do.

☐   People are going to feel sorry for me.

☐   I'm going to sound stupid.

☐   People are not going to take my presentation (or me) seriously.

☐   I'm unprepared.

☐   I'm going to make people feel uncomfortable.

☐   They will hear my voice quaver.

☐   I'm going to come off cold, distant, and unlikeable.

☐   I'm not going to be able to answer the questions they will ask me.

☐   I'm not going to get the promotion (get elected, pass the class, and so on).

2. *Sports Performance*

These statements were taken from athletes, both serious and "weekend," just prior to competition. The names of the actual sports were removed so that you could relate them to any sport or game you choose.

- ☐ I'm going to choke under pressure.
- ☐ I'm going to lose to someone I should beat.
- ☐ I'm going to get hurt.
- ☐ I'm going to make some stupid plays.
- ☐ People will think I don't have any ability.
- ☐ I'm going to forget my training and go back to instinct.
- ☐ I'm going to hurt someone.
- ☐ I'm going to lose money.
- ☐ No one who is decent will want to play with me.
- ☐ I'm going to lose my temper.
- ☐ I'm going to LOSE.

3. *Interviewing for a Job*

These statements were taken from people who were about to go on various types of interviews. Some needed the jobs for survival, some wanted to upgrade their current positions, and some were changing careers.

- ☐ I'm going to misunderstand some of the key questions.
- ☐ I'm either going to say too much or too little.
- ☐ I'm going to wilt under pressure.
- ☐ I'm going to sweat too much.
- ☐ I'm going to appear too desperate.
- ☐ I'm going to dress wrong.
- ☐ I'm going to sound stupid.
- ☐ I'm going to quarrel with the interviewer.

☐ I'm not going to have the right qualifications for the job.

☐ I'm going to give the wrong answers.

☐ I have the wrong image for this job.

☐ I haven't done enough research and preparation for this interview.

4. Singing

I have had many entertainers take my workshops, particularly singers. If you do any type of artistic performing, adapt these items to the type of performing you do. If you do not engage in any form of artistic performance, skip this section.

☐ I'm going to sing off-key.

☐ I'm going to forget the lyrics.

☐ I won't have enough breath support to sing the high notes.

☐ I'm going to move stiffly.

☐ I will not appear warm to the audience.

☐ People will become uncomfortable waiting for my next mistake.

☐ I haven't rehearsed enough.

☐ My performance will be technically adequate, but not artistic or musical.

☐ I'm going to sound amateurish.

☐ I'm not going to "sell" this song.

These sample thoughts should show you the type of thoughts you should be trying to find. Another useful approach to identifying fear-provoking thoughts is *asking yourself key questions.*

One of the reasons a skilled interviewer like Johnny Carson makes so much money is that the right question at the right time can often open up areas of discussion about which even the person being interviewed was unaware. In the next section I will present you with five related questions that will help you sort through and identify your fear-provoking thoughts.

Practice Exercise 5: Questions for Identifying Fear-Provoking Thoughts

Ask yourself each of the following five questions, and record *all* your responses:

1. *What is going to happen when I perform?*

This is the most general question you can ask. If you get lucky enough, it is the only question you will need to ask. If you are having any difficulty getting warmed up, rephrase the question: What might go wrong when I perform? For example, if you are going to talk in front of a large group of people, you will make some predictions about the outcome. If you are anxious about the outcome, some common predictions might be:

- You will forget some part of the talk.

- You will sound disorganized.

- The audience will find you boring.

Write down any predictions that come to mind in the space provided below:

_____

_____

_____

Generally, this first question uncovers a lot of information. It is a good starting point, but will rarely take you far enough. The next four questions represent types of thoughts that can bring about stagefright.

2. *What has happened to me in the past in this type of situation?*

Your history will certainly have a large effect on your predictions about the future. The case study below presents a good illustration.

The Case of Sally C.

Sally C. was a twenty-two-year-old university student in her senior year. She was a music major whose specialty was piano performance. As she was presenting her senior piano recital, which was required of all music performance majors, she developed a problem. She blanked out during the middle of a Chopin sonata, and ran off the recital platform crying.

At the time I met Sally, it had been six months since her recital, and she was still avoiding scheduling another try.

Past experiences, particularly failures, play a very important role in stagefright. You already have some very believable evidence that whatever you are afraid of can happen to you—because it already has! Experience is a great convincer.

When you are answering this question, do not include only what happened, but also write down the consequences. For example, Sally C. didn't pass her senior piano recital, and therefore was not permitted to graduate with her class. Sometimes it is not what happened to you in the past, but the consequences of it that are really worrying you. Write down any experiences, particularly unpleasant ones, in the following space:

_____

_____

_____

3. What have I noticed happen to others in the same situation?

This question is really an extension of the previous one. Observing what happens to other people can be almost as powerful as direct experience. If you have seen someone else do what you are about to do, and have a bad experience at it—even if you have never had such an experience yourself—it might be enough to get you thinking that something like that could happen to you.

In this exercise, don't be too fussy about how similar a situation is to yours. If you have observed people in a situation in which they failed, were embarrassed, or seemed to be humiliated, record it! Don't even limit yourself to situations that you have witnessed personally. If you heard a story about what happened to someone, that story could be influencing you. If nothing comes to mind in this category, make it like a *free association* task and come up with anything you can. It will surprise you to see how easily you can make the connection to your own situation once you have done this. Write these observations in the space below:

_____

_____

_____

4. What is the worst thing that can happen to me in this situation?

This is a more intense version of the previous questions. Again, make sure that you also imagine the *worst* possible consequences of what might happen. Quite often this category is the most fruitful one, particularly for people who tend to be pessimistic or perfectionistic. Anything that *could* happen is fair game. Write your responses in the following space:

_____

_____

_____

5. Secondary questions

Take each negative prediction you have made in response to the previous questions and ask yourself what would happen if it came true. Then take that second prediction and ask again what would happen if it came true, and so on. Here is an example of how this should be done:

Situation: *Asking Judy for a date.*

Negative Prediction: *She'll turn me down.*

And then? *The next time I see her, I'll feel embarrassed.*

And then? *Eventually I'll stop being embarrassed and things will return to normal.*

You can see that in many cases the consequences soon become trivial. Write your secondary questions and answers in the space below:

_____

At this point, you will find it useful to consolidate all the information you have written into one list of fear-provoking thoughts. I will be referring to this list in almost all of the following chapters.

This exercise should have made you fairly anxious. If it did, you are beginning to see that you hold the key to your own relief. If you can learn to control the mechanism that makes you anxious, you can learn to control it so that it will not.

Practice Exercise 6: Getting Yourself Scared

Using the list of fear-provoking thoughts that you have just developed, think of each of them, trying to get yourself anxious. Imagine yourself performing, and experiencing each fearful prediction and its outcome.

In doing this exercise, *imagine everything that could go wrong . . . does!* Do not rush. Take your time developing each image. Try to think of each part as vividly as possible. Try to make out faces and expressions. Try to imagine your reaction to everything that goes on.

Since this book is designed to help you reduce the anxiety around performing, you may be wondering why I deliberately want to get you scared. There are two reasons:

1. There's no better way for you to understand the relationship between thoughts and emotions than to actually induce them through your own controlled thoughts.

2. As you learn to induce anxiety through fear-provoking thoughts, you are actually learning how to control them so that you will also be able to reduce or even eliminate them.

Summary

This chapter clarified the relationship between thoughts and their resulting emotions. As you make a prediction about a performance turning out badly, you will become anxious. Since the cause of stagefright is fear-provoking thoughts about performing poorly and incurring bad consequences, you must learn to identify these thoughts so you can learn to change them.

I reviewed several types of common fear-provoking thoughts that lead to fear in performing, and some methods for identifying them.

4

ANALYZING YOUR
FEAR-PROVOKING THOUGHTS

In this chapter you will determine how reasonable your fear-provoking thoughts are by evaluating the following factors:

1. The situation in which you find yourself

2. The evidence supporting the fear

3. Alternative interpretations

4. The worst possible outcome

5. Logical thinking flaws

Because you believe something is true *does not make it true!* Much of the fear you experience in stagefright comes from beliefs that are either untrue or, if true, greatly exaggerated. If you could learn to get rid of untrue or exaggerated worries, you would greatly reduce the amount of anxiety and fear you experience.

To aid you in determining if your fears are reasonable, I have developed a summary chart to help you keep track of a number of important factors. I will present each area of the chart in a separate section. To use the chart, write one of your fear-provoking thoughts in the first space. Then complete the chart as you read through the rest of this chapter.

Practice Exercise 7:
Fear-Provoking Thought Analysis

1. **Fear-Provoking Thought:**

   _____

2. **Situation:**

   ☐ Center of attention _____

   ☐ Powerful/important audience _____

   ☐ Competent audience _____

   ☐ Strangers in audience _____

   ☐ Family/friends/colleagues in audience _____

   ☐ Novel setting _____

   ☐ New role for you _____

   ☐ Audience size _____

   ☐ Audience fidgeting, bored _____

   ☐ Prominent evaluation _____

   ☐ High level of competition _____

   ☐ Self-esteem on the line _____

3. **Supporting Data:**

   From direct experience _____

   From indirect experience _____

   From rumor _____

4. **Alternative Interpretations:**

   _____

   _____

   _____

   _____

5. Worst Case:

Worst that could happen _____

Worst consequences if it happened _____

How tolerable would consequences be? _____

What could you do to cope? _____

How likely is it that worse will come to worst? _____

6. Logical Flaws:

☐ Overgeneralization

☐ All-or-nothing thoughts

☐ Disqualification of the positive

☐ Magnification

☐ Minimization

☐ Mental filter

7. Reasonableness Rating: _____

0	10	20	30	40	50	60	70	80	90	100

Unreasonable   Uncertain   Reasonable

Situation

I have stressed that stagefright is not a personality trait that some people have and some do not. Stagefright varies with the particular situation and circumstances surrounding any performance situation, whether it is talking before an audience of a thousand people or asking someone for a date. Situational factors and the interpretation of their importance determine how much anxiety you will experience. Below are a number of situational factors that have been found to have a strong influence on stagefright:

Being the Center of Attention

In most cases the closer you are to being the center of attention, the more butterflies you will experience. If you are performing as part of a group, you will generally not experience as much nervousness as when you are performing alone. For example, a member of a musical ensemble usually feels less stagefright than a solo performer.

Audience Characteristics

The composition of the audience can play a large role in determining your level of stagefright. Here are two of the more common influential factors:

Power and status. The more influential the members of the audience, the more likely you will be to experience stagefright. Their effect becomes even stronger if their power or status relates directly to the area of your performance. For example, if you were giving a talk on your company's new marketing policy and a well-known marketing professor from the Harvard Business School was in the audience, your stagefright would be likely to increase.

Competence. The more competent the members of the audience are in your area, the more stagefright you will experience.

The Case of Phillip Q.

Phillip Q. was a classical guitarist in his early twenties. During a rehearsal for a recital, a colleague of mine heard him play a difficult piece flawlessly. The audience for his recital was to be a large group of music teachers. When he finally performed, he was so nervous playing before them that he made over seventy mistakes (that was where my friend stopped counting).

The Amount of Uncertainty in the Situation

The more novel or unfamiliar the situation, the more anxiety you will experience. There are many factors that can influence the uncertainty of a situation. Below are a few of the more important ones:

A strange audience versus a familiar one. People often get more nervous performing before people who know them because a poor performance will be remembered, discussed, or even held up to ridicule. In other cases, people fear performing before strangers.

The novelty of the situation. Usually, the more a situation differs from others in which you have performed, the more stagefright you are likely to experience. For example, a club tennis player may feel very comfortable during a normal tennis match, even with a few spectators. The situation is very different during a tournament with many spectators, a referee, and a person making point-by-point commentary.

Role novelty. As you find yourself in a new and unfamiliar role, your stagefright will probably increase.

The Case of Larry G.

Larry G. was an hourly employee of a local company who was promoted to the position of supervisor. He became very nervous whenever he had to address his "old buddies" in meetings he had to conduct.

Audience Size

If you are like most people, the larger the audience, the more stagefright you will experience.

Your Sensitivity to Other's Reactions

The more sensitive you are to the reactions of the audience, the more stagefright you will experience. If you were giving a talk and you noticed people beginning to whisper to each other, or beginning to stare around the room, you might get anxious. The more you interpreted these actions as signs of disinterest in your presentation, the more stagefright you would experience.

The Prominence of an Evaluation

The more obvious it is to you that you are being evaluated, the more likely you are to experience stagefright. If your performance were being videotaped, or there were judges in the audience with clipboards and pencils, you would probably get a lot more nervous than if they were just sitting there as passive observers.

The Level of Competition

If you are in direct competition with someone through your performance, you will probably experience more stagefright.

The Consequences of the Evaluation for Self-Esteem

If the area of your performance is very important in determining how you feel about yourself, you will be more likely to experience stagefright. If you took an acting class for fun and tried out for a play, you might feel quite a bit less pressured during the audition than a serious actor to whom getting the part might be a reflection of self-worth and value.

Supporting Data

Here I want you to examine the validity of the evidence supporting your fear-provoking thoughts. Quite often, people think themselves into becoming anxious, but they do not have any evidence that supports the fear-provoking prediction they have made. Alice H., our high school teacher, provides a good example.

The Case of Alice H. (Cont'd.)

Alice believed that she would become disorganized when she presented a seminar paper to her class. One of the reasons she remained nervous was that she never questioned her predictions to see if they were well-founded. When I interviewed her, it turned out that *she had never actually gotten disorganized while speaking in public.* When I pushed her harder, she recalled seeing one of her friends in a seminar class get lost during a talk. Alice became very embarrassed for her friend. *That* was the only evidence supporting her fear-provoking thoughts. Once she realized that there was very little evidence to support her fears, she gave them up quickly.

For the fear-provoking thought on the summary chart, identify the data you are using to support it. The data will come from one of three sources:

1. *Direct experience.* The event you predicted or the consequence of it had actually happened to you personally.

2. *Indirect experience.* Either it has happened to someone you know, or you have had contact with someone who had directly observed it.

3. *Rumor.* You have heard about it, but you were not in contact with the actual source who was witness to it.

Make the strongest supporting case possible for your fear-provoking thought. Include dates, places, times, names, and so on. Then examine the supporting data you have identified and determine if you really think that it is strong enough evidence to warrant your being upset.

The next three sections will show you additional ways to evaluate the supporting evidence you have identified.

Alternative Interpretations

As I have mentioned throughout this book, people rarely differentiate between facts and interpretations. Predictions are treated as truth. One really good way to combat such tyranny of thinking is to come up with one or more alternative interpretations for your fear-provoking thought. When you can identify alternative interpretations that are plausible, you will begin to question your interpretations instead of blindly accepting them as truth.

The Case of Rod R.

Rod R. was a young attorney who was afraid to approach women and ask them on a date. Rod believed that women found him unattractive, and therefore would always reject him. Each time he was rejected, he knew why: unattractiveness.

I asked Rod, "If you approached a woman and she didn't seem interested, could there be any other reason besides your attractiveness, or lack of it?" Rod looked at me as if I were from Mars, and told me there were certain things that were facts. He pointed to a chair and said, "chair." He pointed to a desk and said, "desk." He pointed to himself and said, "unattractive." He told me there was no room here for interpretations—this was a fact. If a woman rejected him, there was only one reason for it: unattractiveness.

I asked him to imagine that he walked up to a woman alone at a table in a restaurant and began talking to her and she was not interested. As a warm-up, I began with a few far-fetched interpretations:

- Suppose that she had just been released from a rape clinic an hour ago and you were the first man she talked to. If she was not interested, could it be for any other reason than your level of attractiveness? He said, "Well, maybe in this *one* case." I continued.

- Suppose the next woman was married to a very jealous man who beat her whenever he caught her talking to another man. The jealous husband was in the next room talking on the restaurant pay phone while you were trying to talk to her. Is her reluctance caused by your unattractiveness? He said, "Well . . . maybe not in this case either." I tried still another.

- This time you try to strike up a conversation with a woman who, unbeknownst to you, believes that all men are filthy beasts who only want three things (which will not be printed here). She is currently finishing her latest book urging mandatory celibacy for all civil servants. By this time he got the point!

By forming alternative interpretations it is easier to understand that your view is not a fact, just one of several views of a situation. More importantly, if your interpretation is unreasonable, you will be more likely to see it as such after considering other views of the situation.

The Case of Cheryl M.

Cheryl M. had a bad experience giving a talk to her staff about the next two years' projected goals. She was quite anxious during the talk. She attributed her poor performance to the fact that she was a poor public speaker who always got nervous in front of a group. When pushed to provide alternative explanations, here are a few she listed:

- She did not have time to prepare adequately.

- The projected goals were given to her in a very vague fashion by the vice-president.

- She presented the talk at 4:45 on a Friday afternoon when everyone was thinking about trying to beat the traffic going home for the weekend.

Just thinking about the alternative explanations that she identified made her feel better. She realized that there were some very concrete reasons for her poor talk besides her public speaking ability.

If you find it difficult to come up with alternative explanations and seem to be locked into seeing the situation in only one way, it is very likely that your thought, or interpretation, is unreasonable. Ask someone to help you generate some alternative interpretations.

Worst Case

In the previous chapter you were asked to identify the worst thing that could happen during your performance, and the worst possible consequence that could result from it. In this section you will continue that process by answering the following five questions:

1. What is the worst thing that could happen during your performance?

_____

_____

_____

2. What is the worst possible consequence if the above happened?

_____

_____

_____

3. How tolerable would those worst case outcomes be?

_____

_____

_____

4. What could you do to cope when *worse comes to worst?*

_____

_____

_____

5. How likely is it that *worse will come to worst?*

_____

_____

_____

By doing this analysis, you have still another way to determine how reasonable your fears are. The worst case analysis can reveal much useful information. It can show you that the chances of something really bad happening are remote. Also, you may often realize that the consequences for a bad outcome are not really catastrophic, and are certainly bearable. Finally, the worst case analysis can show that you will be able to cope with the consequences of even the worst possible outcome.

Logical Flaws

The way you think when you are upset is often different from the way you think at other times. People who think themselves into stage-fright often *bend* logic to do it. Learning to identify these logical flaws is another way to discover when your fears are unreasonable. Based on his work with Aaron Beck, David Burns identified several logical thinking flaws and presented them in his 1980 book *Feeling Good*. In this section I will explain five of these logical flaws that are common among people who experience stagefright. Then you can examine the data supporting your fear-provoking thoughts and determine if any of these logical flaws are present.

Overgeneralization

You may have had a bad experience during a performance. As a result, if you now think that all future performances will turn out the same way, you are *overgeneralizing*. Typically, overgeneralizing requires very little data in order to reach a conclusion. A key to identifying overgeneralization is to look for the words *always* and *never*.

The Case of Sally C. (Revisited)

Sally C. was the music student who ran off the stage crying during her senior recital. She had blanked out and forgotten the piece she was playing. Based on that *one* incident, she was sure that she would never be able to remember under pressure again.

All-or-Nothing Thoughts

This is thinking in extremes without admitting the possibility of a middle ground. The world usually looks quite gray—rarely is anything pure black or white.

The Case of John T.

John T. was a college tennis player. He believed that there were only two types of tennis players: great ones and awful ones. Great ones were any players who could beat him. Terrible ones were those he could beat. He would get very nervous whenever he had to play one of the great ones because they were so much better than he was.

Things are rarely this way in the world. Are all your friends wonderful people or are they all terrible? Is your car a Rolls Royce or a broken-down wreck? Is your office perfectly organized or is it in chaos? Evaluating things as either black or white is unreasonable. You will not either forget every part of your speech or remember every detail perfectly all the time.

Disqualification of the Positive

This is basing a conclusion on poor or no information, in spite of evidence to the contrary. When people hold an idea about themselves, they often look for evidence to support it. If the evidence does not support it, they will distort the evidence until it fits their point of view. Below is an example of a man who believed that people could always tell when he was nervous. He believed his anxiety symptoms were so strong that everybody had to be aware of them, regardless of what they told him.

The Case of Ernie A.

Ernie A. was a marketing coordinator who did not want people to see how nervous he got during staff meetings. The people in those meetings actually complimented him about how calm and self-assured he always appeared in front of the group. He disregarded this feedback from others and continued to believe that his nervousness was always detectable by everyone. He distorted the compliments and said, "If I didn't look so nervous, they wouldn't feel obligated to try and compliment me."

Magnification (Catastrophizing) or Minimization

Here you magnify your failures and fears out of proportion, while minimizing your triumphs and strong points. There is a tendency to dwell on the negative no matter how small it is. Positive factors are ignored or their role is de-emphasized. Below is an example of a comedian who ignored all his successes every time he had even the slightest setback.

The Case of Jim Y.

Jim Y. was a young comedian who had just completed a week of performing at a local comedy nightclub when he came to see me. He was terrified to go back on stage because he had failed so badly during his one-week engagement. I discovered that he had been enormously successful for six out of seven nights. On one of the nights, however, his reception was lukewarm. All he could talk about when asked how his week had gone was how badly he had done based on that one night's poor performance. When his friends pointed out how well he had done on the other six nights, he dismissed those performances and talked only about his one off night.

Mental Filter

A mental filter is the operation of taking an idea out of context and basing a conclusion on it while ignoring other valid information. The idea that is taken out of context may be inconsequential, yet there is still a tendency to dwell on it. The following is an example of a man who was given a suggestion for making his presentations more effective. He took the suggestion to mean that his presentation was rotten.

The Case of Ernest K.

Ernest K. was a district sales manager who conducted a meeting that his supervisor attended. At the end, his supervisor complimented him on the efficient and organized way he had run the meeting. Then he mentioned that he thought Ernest could become even more effective by duplicating sales figures and passing them out a day or two before. Ernest took the suggestion to mean that his *entire* meeting had been a failure based on the *one* suggestion made by the boss.

When you are employing a mental filter, all contrary evidence that does not support a particular view is rejected, or "filtered" out. In examining the supporting data for your fear-provoking thought, see if you have omitted any relevant data because it did not seem to fit. Look for key words such as *always* or *never*. Check to see how well the evidence really supports your fear-provoking thought.

Reasonableness Rating

Now that you have gone through the first six categories on the chart, you are ready to make an *overall reasonableness rating*. This is simply done by rereading all the entries you have made on your chart and then determining, on a 0-to-100 scale, how reasonable you think your fear-provoking thoughts really are.

This is your time to become critical and tough. Examine each category on your chart and try to detect any instances of bias, distortion, or illogic.

Evaluating Your Rating

If your rating is from 0 to 20 for each of your major fear-provoking thoughts, and the process of analysis has in itself considerably reduced your fear of performing, congratulations. You can probably skip the next chapter and go on to chapter six, which covers goal setting.

If your ratings of fear-provoking thoughts tend to be in the 30 to 70 range, you're still uncertain about how reasonable your fears are. Continue on to the next chapter. It will help you in two ways: by providing further ways of testing your thoughts for reasonableness and by showing how to use affirming self-statements to cope with fear-provoking thoughts that persist.

If your ratings of fear-provoking thoughts are in the 80 to 100 range and they still seem quite reasonable, you will benefit greatly from the reality-testing techniques in the next chapter. This will be the acid test that will either confirm your fears or prove them to be unfounded to some degree. If it turns out that your fear-provoking thoughts are indeed reasonable, you should concentrate on relaxation techniques, affirmations, goal setting, and extra rehearsal to minimize the effects of your thoughts.

The Case of Janet D.

Janet D. is a stock and bond broker who is about to make a major sales presentation to a group of wealthy investors. She has been trying to get in to make this presentation for five months. If she succeeds, it would be worth a great deal of money.

Here is how Janet completed her analysis of her most fear-provoking thought:

Fear-Provoking Thought Analysis

1. Fear-Provoking Thought:

They are going to doubt my competence because I'm a woman.

2. Situation:

- ☐ Center of attention: *only presenter*
- ☐ Powerful/important audience: *big bucks*
- ☐ Competent audience: *well-informed investors*
- ☐ Strangers in audience: *total strangers*
- ☐ Family/friends/colleagues in audience: *none*
- ☐ Novel setting: *have made presentations before*
- ☐ New role for you: *role same*
- ☐ Audience size: *24*
- ☐ Audience: *fidgeting, bored*
- ☐ Prominent evaluation: *very prominent*
- ☐ High level of competition: *very competitive*
- ☐ Self-esteem on the line: *as a professional*

3. Supporting Data:

From direct experience: *Thought I lost some past sales because of gender.*

From indirect experience: *Female friend got negative feedback from aerospace audience based on gender.*

From rumor: *Read articles about discrimination against females.*

4. Alternative Interpretations:

Pay more attention because I'm a woman. They will evaluate competence, not gender. They will want to impress me because I am a woman.

5. Worst Case:

Worst that could happen: *Make no sale and damage reputation.*

Worst consequences if it happened: *Would lose many current sales.*

How tolerable would consequences be? *Very unpleasant.*

What could you do to cope? *Organize and rehearse. Talk with successful salespeople who work with similar groups.*

How likely is it that worse will come to worst? *Unlikely.*

6. Logical Flaws:

- ☐ Overgeneralization
- ☐ All-or-nothing thoughts
- ☐ Disqualification of the positive
- ☐ Magnification
- ☐ Minimization
- ☐ Mental filter

7. Reasonableness Rating: _____

0	10	20	30	40	50	60	70	80	90	100
Unreasonable					Uncertain				Reasonable	

Summary

In this chapter I have proceeded step by step through an analysis of major fear-provoking thoughts:

1. Stating the thought

2. Assessing the situation

3. Listing supporting data

4. Devising alternative interpretations

5. Extrapolating the worst case

6. Identifying logical flaws

7. Rating the thought for reasonableness

5

COPING WITH FEAR-PROVOKING THOUGHTS

This chapter is divided into two parts: reality testing methods for thoughts that still seem reasonable, and composing affirming self-statements to cope with thoughts that, however unreasonable, still persist.

Reality Testing

Sometimes it is difficult to judge the reasonableness of your fear-provoking thoughts. It is important to remember that these judgments represent interpretations of facts rather than being facts themselves. As you have discovered, there are times when the data itself is insufficient to permit a clear determination of reasonableness. When that is the case, you can do what psychologists call *reality testing*. You assume the role of a *scientist* and actually see if your thoughts hold up under rigorous scientific investigation. You will get to use your favorite laboratory—yourself. I will present two methods for testing out the reasonableness of your thoughts: suspending judgment and shame-attacking.

Suspending Judgment

This method is a universal technique used by clinical psychologists. It has been fashionable since the early 1960s when research on creativity showed that creative people had the ability to suspend judgment and tolerate ambiguity. In *suspending judgment* to combat stagefright, the main idea is to avoid evaluating your performance, and continually act *as though* you were not afraid. Here are two ways to do this:

Use your own "unafraid" behavior as a model. The first step here is to identify some related performance area where you are not hampered by fear-provoking thoughts and you do not experience stagefright. I used this method with Alice H., our high school biology teacher.

The Case of Alice H. (Final Visit)

Alice H. was the biology teacher who felt very comfortable speaking before thirty high school students, but experienced fear when presenting seminar papers before small groups of students and her professor. I asked Alice to figure out why she felt unafraid in front of her own classes, and she gave the following reasons:

- She believed that she knew much more about the topic than anyone else in the room.

- If she did say anything that was incorrect (which she knew she would not do, but if she ever did), there would be no serious consequences.

- She was confident that her students knew her and liked her.

Alice agreed to suspend her judgment about the scariness of her seminar class, and to act in her seminar class as if she were in her own biology class. This reduced her fear considerably. She realized that she was a good student, and had researched her seminar topic well enough so that she would not make any dumb mistakes. She certainly had become more of an expert in it than her classmates. She also realized that she was not expected to know more than her professor, and that the likelihood of terrible consequences for a slight slip were very low.

Use successful role models. Act as if you were someone else whom you respect a great deal. Take on that person's confidence, poise, and charm. Use the same jokes, gestures, and turns of phrase. Make the same kinds of decisions.

Shame-Attacking

Shame-attacking exercises were developed by Albert Ellis, the founder of Rational Emotive Therapy. They are very useful for testing fear-provoking thoughts that seem reasonable. Here are the steps to follow for performing a shame-attacking exercise:

1. Identify something you could do that would embarrass or shame you a great deal. Try to find an action that would produce maximum stagefright for you.

2. Predict what the results would be if you did this thing that would embarrass you. Be as detailed in your prediction as possible so that you can use this prediction for a comparison with what actually happens later.

3. After identifying the prediction, actually do the action!

4. Compare the *actual* results with the *predicted* results. See how accurate or inaccurate your prediction was.

There is no better way to get rid of an unreasonable fear-provoking thought then to test it out and show how wrong your initial prediction was.

The Case of Peter D.

Years ago, I was attending a practicum led by (*the author*) Ellis. Each participant was given the task of performing a shame-attacking exercise. Ellis had given examples of people doing silly things such as walking a banana along the street on a leash, and riding in a crowded New York elevator and calling out each floor.

On the third day of the practicum, I was having lunch with three other practicum members. Two of them, Pam and Marcie, decided they were going to perform their shame-attacking exercise during lunch. Pam announced that she was going to perform her shame-attacking exercise by standing up after she had eaten her lunch and singing "Happy Birthday" to Marcie. Furthermore, she requested that the rest of our party remain silent, which would increase her shame.

Marcie said that if Pam had the nerve to sing "Happy Birthday" to her in the restaurant, the least she could do was to make a short acceptance speech—which would be her shame-attacking exercise. They both agreed that they would find these acts extremely embarrassing, and would fulfill the requirements of the exercise.

I told Pam and Marcie that their choices were not appropriate for this exercise. I also mentioned that the song and speech were too contrived and theatrical, and not really personally embarrassing for them. After the two women got through calling me names that are not reprintable, they assured me that their exercises were quite appropriate.

At that point, my immediate thought was, "OK, if they want to act foolish, let 'em. I'll just wait in the restroom until they're done." Then I suddenly realized, I was trying to persuade them not to do their shame-attacking exercises because *they would embarrass me!* I decided that for my own shame-attacking exercise *I would sit through the entire ordeal—no matter how terrible or embarrassing it would be for me.*

The first task in doing a shame-attacking exercise was to decide on a task. Since that was done, the next step was to make a prediction about what would happen if the exercise was carried out. My prediction was that *everyone at the restaurant would ignore Pam and Marcie and stare at me. They would all think, "How could a guy like him be with people like that?"*

Pam got up and sang. If she was not nervous, then she gave a very good imitation of a nervous person. Her hands were trembling and her voice was breaking. Interestingly, a few other people at nearby tables began singing along with her. When they noticed that no one else at our table was singing, they stopped and turned away, looking awkward and embarrassed. During all this, I looked around and noticed that I appeared to be invisible. No one seemed to notice that I was even there.

I quickly got angry with myself. I thought about all the thousands of times that I had stopped myself from doing things I wanted to do because of what people might think about me, even strangers . . . especially strangers.

Practice Exercise 8:
Practicing a Shame-Attacking Exercise

Design your own shame-attacking exercise. Consider this as a free trial or excuse to do something daring, something you've always wanted to do. *Now it is therapeutic.* Complete each of the items below in detail:

1. Describe the task you will perform:

_____

_____

_____

2. Make a prediction about the outcome of the task:

_____

_____

_____

3. Actually carry out the task!

_____

_____

_____

4. Describe the actual results of carrying out the task:

_____

_____

_____

Compare your prediction with the actual results, and determine if your prediction was reasonable or not.

Affirming Self-Statements

Now that you have determined that some of your fear-provoking thoughts may be unreasonable, I will deal with some techniques for learning how to contend with them. You may already have discovered that just by the act of labeling your thoughts as unreasonable, the fears they produce are diminished. Of course, many times additional work is needed.

Since fear-provoking thoughts are really internal dialogues, or "talking to yourself," I will use affirming self-statements to help you cope with them. This does not mean that you will now be asked to walk around chanting pat slogans like, "Every day I'm getting better." Your self-statements will come from the self-analysis you have been conducting in the previous chapters.

By now you have already discovered how habitual and automatic your thoughts are. Quite often you have the skills that would enable you to cope with a difficult situation, but for some reason they are not used. Sometimes they are just temporarily forgotten under the stress of the moment. Affirming self-statements can serve as reminders to use skills you already have.

You have learned how easy it is for you to predict doom for an impending performance. By selecting and rehearsing appropriately affirming self-statements, you will remind yourself of the unreasonableness of some of your fear-provoking thoughts. For example, Joe H., an aerospace engineer, always worried that something would go wrong when he was asked to make a presentation to governmental review agencies. He had an unreasonable fear of leaving out minute details. He decided to cure himself by using the phrase "Focus on the big picture." This reminded him of his unreasonable preoccupation with details.

Refuting Unreasonable Thoughts

Affirming self-statements are the distilled results of refuting unreasonable thoughts. Once you have discovered why a particular fear-provoking thought is unreasonable, the affirming self-statement is used as a reminder. The real work is done in the act of refutation. Below are the steps you should proceed through to refute an unreasonable fear-provoking thought:

1. Realistically appraise the situation. The Fear-Provoking Thought Analysis form you used in the last chapter can be used as a guide to help you examine the situational elements of your fear-provoking thoughts. Try to identify any aspects of the situation that contradict your fear-provoking thoughts. For example, if you are predicting failure, try to remember similar situations in which you performed well. Here are some sample self-statements based on the situation:

> *I know more than this audience.*
> *I've done this before.*
> *These people want me to succeed.*
> *Disregard the fidgeters.*
> *I like myself whether I do well or poorly.*

2. Identify weaknesses of the supporting data. There are two things to look for here: the amount of data and its strength. For example, in the case of Janet D. there was very little data to support her assumption about sex-discrimination. She had only the report of one friend talking about one instance. From that she generalized to all cases for herself.

Because people believe their own experience more than anything else, it is very important to examine it in relationship to fear-provoking thoughts. You should always determine if your experience bears directly on the situation, and if it really supports the fear-provoking thoughts. Here are some examples:

> *There's no proof I'll fail.*
> *This is a fresh start—the past has no bearing.*
> *My fear is based only on rumor and hearsay.*
> *No overgeneralizations.*

3. Identifying alternative interpretations. Once Janet D. saw new, alternative interpretations for her fear-provoking thoughts, it became much easier for her to face her audience. As she saw possibilities for having gender be a neutral, or even beneficial, factor, her confidence level rose. Here are some alternative interpretations:

> *If they yawn, it could be from insomnia the night before.*
> *There are lots of reasons for leaving early.*
> *Who knows why people do things? I don't.*
> *No mindreading.*

4. Surviving the worst case. Worse rarely comes to worst, but even if it did, most people would end up distressed rather than destroyed. Janet D. realized that even if she gave a terrible presentation, things would not end in disaster. It is true that she would not get what she wanted out of that situation, but she realized there would be other opportunities. It was important for her to identify other success-ful brokers whom she had seen give bad presentations. Here are some sample reminders:

> *I'll survive this.*
> *Distress is not disaster.*
> *No big deal here.*
> *If all else fails, I'm still alive.*

5. Identifying logical flaws. Go over the list of logical flaws in the previous chapter and determine which ones you have indulged in. Each time you can identify a logical flaw you become better at detecting them and eventually in avoiding them. Janet D. had a strong tendency to overgeneralize from very small amounts of data. Eventually, she learned how to identify when there was enough data to justify a fear-provoking thought. She spent a lot less time being anxious. Here are some rational refutations of logical flaws:

> *One snowflake doesn't make a blizzard.*
> *Stay in the gray area.*
> *Accentuate the positive, not the negative.*
> *Keep things in perspective.*
> *Listen without judgment. Look and learn.*

6. Reminding yourself of your skills and preparation. Com-pose self-statements that reinforce the relaxation skills you have ac-quired, the goals you have set, and the presentation techniques you have practiced. For example:

> *Remember to breathe.*
> *I can close my eyes for a second and relax.*
> *My outline is right here.*
> *I've done this six times in front of the mirror.*
> *Pause and ask for questions.*
> *I can summarize my main points at the end.*

Practice Exercise 9: Designing Affirming Self-Statements

Once you have been able to refute your fear-provoking thoughts, the important thing is to learn to use the results of those refutations. If you refute a fear-provoking thought then forget about it, you have done yourself little good. In this section take the essence of each refutation and form affirmative self-statements.

There are a few simple rules to follow in designing your affirming self-statements:

1. *The statements should be short and simple.* They would do you little good if you could not remember them.

2. *They should be stated in positive form.* They will be a bit more inspiring for you if they remind you of what heights you can lift yourself to, rather than what depths you might fall into if you are not careful. For example, "I can do this" is better than "I am not failing."

3. *They should be stated in the present tense.* Affirming self-statements are designed to help you at the moment, not at some distant point in the future. Also, your unconscious mind operates in a constant present, making no distinction between past, present, and future.

4. *They should be stated in the first person.* This will help to remind you about the control you have over your own behavior.

Using Affirming Self-Statements

Once you have designed a set of appropriate affirming self-statements, it is important to know how and when to use them. Here are some suggestions for their use:

1. Always use affirming self-statements as you practice for any performance. This way, you not only practice the talk itself, but you also practice invoking and using the affirming self-statements.

2. Use affirming self-statements as you practice relaxation training exercises. By doing this you will associate the state of relaxation with the affirming self-statements, which will increase the calming effect that they have for you.

3. Use any type of reminder that you can to cue yourself to practice them. Whether it is pink post-it notes on the bathroom mirror or wearing a rubber band around your wrist as a reminder, find ways to cue yourself to practice.

Summary

In this chapter I have presented some ways for you to cope with fear-provoking thoughts. They included reality-testing exercises such as suspending judgment and shame-attacking, plus how to refute fear-provoking thoughts then construct and use affirming self-statements.

6

GOAL SETTING

In this chapter you will learn the principles of good goal setting and set *your* goals for controlling stagefright.

There are three major principles in setting reasonable goals for yourself:

1. Set goals that are directly under your control. Express your goals in terms of your own conscious actions, not the actions and reactions of others.

2. Base goals on your list of fear-provoking thoughts, making sure that your goals will help lead to their reduction or elimination.

3. Be specific so that you can recognize when you have successfully met your goals. State your goals in terms of discrete actions, quantities, dates, and times. Break large, complex goals down into small, distinct steps—what you are going to do today, tomorrow, and next week. This removes ambiguity and makes it easy to gauge your progress toward a particular goal.

These principles are easier to prevent by way of examples.

The Case of Judy S.

Judy S. was informed that she was one of three final candidates to be interviewed for the position of controller of a large corporation. This was the opportunity she had been working toward for several years. When the interview finally came, she was very nervous.

Her answers to questions were vague and unfocused. She did not present an effective and organized presentation of her past experience and qualifications. She felt so ill-at-ease that she thought her personality did not come across to the interview team.

She came to see me a few weeks before another major interview. When I asked what her goals were for the interview, she said, "Goals? I only have one goal: to land the job of controller."

I pointed out to Judy that getting the job was an unreasonable goal because it was *not directly under her control*. There was nothing she could do that would *guarantee* her getting the job. To help formulate her goals, I began by identifying her fear-provoking thoughts. Using her previous experience, she identified four issues that were worrying her:

1. She was afraid that the interview committee would think that she was disorganized.

2. She was afraid that she would not be thought of as sharp and fast on her feet in responding to questions.

3. She was afraid that the committee would not get a sense of "who she was."

4. She was afraid that she would not get the job.

Identifying these fears was a good beginning, but they were all based on events that were not under her control. The next step was to *translate* these fear-provoking thoughts into specific actions she could take. These actions would all have to be directly under her control. Each of these actions, when taken, would lower her fears and help bring about what she wanted. I helped her set the following goals:

1. Appearing More Organized

Outline and edit her relevant prior experience and qualifications for the job. Although Judy could not control how well organized she appeared to the committee, there were things she could do to remove her worries about not being organized. With a concise outline of her experience and qualifications, she would be able to walk into the room confident that when she was asked about her background, she could make a clear, well-organized response. To help meet this goal, Judy broke it down into several subgoals:

- After she finished editing her outline, she would show it to three colleagues who had served on similar interviewing committees.

- Once the outline was finished, Judy would practice saying it while driving to and from work, until she could deliver it smoothly.

2. Responding to Questions

Ask three experienced colleagues for sample questions so that she could practice responding in a simulated interview. Again, she added two subgoals here:

- Judy worked out a format for responding to questions. If she had a good, ready answer, she would pause for a few seconds to organize it, then respond. If it was a difficult question for which she did not have a prepared answer, she would first compliment the interviewer for posing such a challenging question, then she would try to relate it to something she did have prepared. Finally, if all else failed, she would admit to not knowing the answer, but outline how she would go about getting the answer. This would show command of her resources.

- She decided to ask a group of experienced colleagues to give her a "mock" interview so she could practice responding "under fire."

3. Revealing Her Personality

Prepare a series of anecdotes and stories that would reveal something personal to the committee. This made her feel more confident, because she could now focus on the conversation, looking for an opportunity to insert one of her anecdotes. She now believed that she would be able to present herself as she wanted to be viewed.

4. Getting the Job

Judy decided that if she could meet the first three goals she had set, she would have done as much to get the job as possible.

Stating and achieving specific goals that were under her direct control enabled Judy to complete her second interview with a greatly lowered anxiety level. Judy did not get the job, but she was individually complimented by two of the three interviewers on her performance. She later found out that the job was awarded to a relation of one of the board members. She did get a job as controller for a large company on the next try.

The Case of Bill H.

Bill H. was an investment analyst. He was going to make a presentation, with slides, to a group of investment counselors and accountants. If he succeeded, he would earn a great deal of money. If he failed, his colleagues and clients would spread the word about his ineffectiveness, which could lead to his financial ruin. He worried about the presentation for weeks. He arranged and rearranged the order of the slides. He kept on worrying about which suit and tie to wear. During the final four nights, he got very little sleep.

When he finally began making his presentation, it started out adequately. By the third slide, he forgot the slide order. He announced the wrong slide several times, which drew laughs from his audience. He began to get nervous, and lost his place, then began tripping over his words. Several times his talk was interrupted by questions, and again he lost his place. He got progressively more anxious as the talk went on. He fondly reported it as "the second worst afternoon of my life."

When I asked Bill what his goals were for the talk, he told me that they were to inform and impress his audience (not necessarily in that order). In asking him how he prepared to meet these goals, he said that he "spent a lot of time thinking about" what he would say. Bill's actions were typical of people who experience fear and anxiety when speaking before an audience. Fortunately for him, he had another, similar talk scheduled within a few weeks of coming to me.

It was easy to get him to identify his anxiety-provoking thoughts. He believed that in his next talk, the following would probably occur:

1. He would appear disorganized. This disorganization would appear in the form of losing his place and mixing up the slide order again.

2. He would not be able to answer the questions put to him by the audience. This would make him look stupid.

3. He would, once again, trip over his own words, and sound inarticulate.

4. He would appear so useless that his boss would fire him.

The next step was to have Bill set some goals so that he could tell if his approach was successful. His initial fear was that he would appear disorganized to the audience. Setting a goal of appearing organized to the audience was unreasonable, because he could not control their evaluations of his talk. Fortunately, there were several things Bill could do that were directly under his control. These things would make *appearing organized to the audience* much more likely.

1. Appearing Organized

Bill decided to set some very concrete goals that involved writing out his organization on paper, so that he could refer to it should he get very nervous. This would ensure that he could not get too disorganized, because the organization was always available to him directly. He planned the following steps:

*   Prepare a list of slides so that he would not forget their order. If he did forget the next slide, he would only have to glance down at his notes.

*   Prepare an outline of his talk. If he was interrupted by a question, a glance at his outline would let him know where he was. He added a list of key words to help him remember to include important topics, anecdotes, and examples.

2. Answering All Questions

The next fear, about being unable to answer every question put to him by the audience, was also one that Bill could not control directly. There was no way to *guarantee* that he would be able to answer every question regardless of the preparation he went through. He decided to use consultation to help him reduce these fear-provoking thoughts.

Bill set the goal of asking his boss and several veteran colleagues about the questions that were likely to be asked by this type of audience. He also set the goal of asking what sources he could read up on to prepare for the talk, and of course the goal of doing the actual reading in preparation.

In his consultation, he also asked for their opinions about how to handle those questions he still could not answer. He was told to respond as follows:

- Begin with an admission that he did not know the answer.

- Ask if anyone in the audience knew the answer.

- If they did, thank them and *offer them a job* (or some other suitable joke to lighten the situation). If no one knew the answer, tell the person asking the question that it was a good one, and that he would research it and get back to him or her with the answer.

3. *Sounding Articulate*

The next fear was that he would trip over his words and sound inarticulate. Again, there is no way to ensure smooth speech in front of an audience, but there were things for Bill to do to make it more likely to happen.

Bill agreed to finish preparing his speech several days before the actual presentation date. This gave him time to actually practice saying his speech aloud. He used this opportunity to get used to any difficult words or phrases, and get into the flow of the talk. He practiced his talk into a cassette recorder to get feedback, identify rough spots that needed more practice, and know his talk better by listening to the playback.

By the time we got to the last fear-provoking thought . . . being fired, Bill realized that it certainly was not directly under his control. Furthermore, he realized that if he met the other three goals he set, the likelihood of being fired was not great enough to worry about.

Goal Setting for Sports

A few years ago, I ran a stagefright workshop for athletes. I asked the participants to identify their goals when performing their sport. Here are a few of the responses I received:

- I want to win the match.

- I want to be one of the first fifty finishers in the 10K race.

- I want to strike out Jim.

- I want to serve at least ten aces in my next match.

- I want to make my coach proud of me.

These seem to be fairly obvious goals, but they all contain a major flaw. They cannot be directly controlled. Here is one example to help drive this point home:

The Case of Don K.

Don K. was an investment banker with a passion for tennis. He belonged to a tennis club, and played no less than three times a week. It was Don who said that he wanted to serve ten aces in a tennis match. (An ace is a tennis serve that is hit so well that it wins the point without the opponent touching it with his or her racquet.)

Here are a few obstacles—beyond Don's control—that could keep him from obtaining his goal, even though he was serving very well:

- His opponent might be too good! He could be able to return the best serves Don is capable of hitting.

- A gust of wind could affect his toss, ruining his serve.

- His opponent might cheat, and make a bad line-call on a close serve.

- Just as Don is about to hit a serve, he could be distracted by a sudden, loud noise.

In each of the cases presented above, Don could do everything as well as it could possibly be done, but still fail to achieve his goal. In each example, the obstacle causing him to fail is not under his control.

Furthermore, although I listed only four things that could have gone wrong, the potential list is endless, as all tennis players who have ever lost a match know.

When people set unreasonable goals and do *not* reach them, they feel bad. This may come out in the form of anger, depression, or anxiety. Now here is the problem: *They may have done everything they could, but in their view, it was not enough!* This leaves them with the unreasonable attitude that *they should have done more.* A guaranteed way to make yourself feel bad is to insist that you have done everything that you could, *but you should have done more.*

I'm not saying that Don was wrong to want to hit aces, but I am saying that it was an unreasonable goal. If he wanted to hit aces, some more reasonable goals would have been the following ones:

- Relax before serving, and concentrate.

- Toss the ball straight and high.

- Take a full backswing.

- Keep the head up, watching the ball while swinging.

If Don had achieved each of the goals above, he might still not have served any aces. Achieving each of the goals above, however, would make the goal of serving an ace much more likely. Furthermore, each of these goals is a skill that can be practiced, while "hitting aces" cannot. This gives Don a great deal of control over achieving each of his goals.

Below is a short exercise designed to give you the opportunity to practice discriminating between goals that are under your control and those that are not.

Practice Exercise 10:
Identifying Controllable Goals

A man is about to go out on a job interview. He has set the following six goals below. Identify each as an example of a goal that is

Directly under his control: by placing a "C" in the space provided, or

Not directly under his control: by placing an "N" in the space provided.

Goals

_____ 1. To make sure he is not misunderstood on key points during an interview.

_____ 2. To ask at least three knowledgeable friends or colleagues to make comments on the appropriateness of the clothes he intends to wear on a job interview.

_____ 3. To keep his voice from quavering during the interview.

_____ 4. To get the job.

_____ 5. To impress the interviewers with his ability to "think on his feet."

_____ 6. Get information about the company he is interviewing with.

Answers to Practice Exercise 10

1. N—Although you can do a variety of things to make being misunderstood less likely, you cannot control how well your audience will understand you.

2. C—You cannot control whether an interviewer will think that you have dressed appropriately, but you can get good advice from informed friends and colleagues. Such advice will make dressing appropriately more likely.

3. N—You cannot directly control the amount of quaver in your voice when you are anxious, although you can practice relaxation exercises so that you are more likely not to present this symptom of anxiety.

4. N—Getting the job is not under your control. You may give a dazzling interview, but the job was already promised to the boss's prospective son-in-law (if he goes through with the wedding).

5. N—You cannot control what others think of your performance. You can only control doing your best, then hope. . . .

6. C—This one is totally under your control. Most prospective employers are favorably impressed when a candidate comes to the interview having done his or her homework. This is a

way of showing that you are sincerely interested in a career with the company rather than just getting a job.

Practice Exercise 11:
Setting Your Own Goals

Now that you know how to set goals that are under your control, it is time for you to set a few. Using *two* of the fear-provoking thoughts you have identified from the previous chapters, set a goal or series of goals that *you could* accomplish to reduce each particular worry.

Fear 1: _____

    Goals: _____

        _____

        _____

        _____

        _____

Fear 2: _____

    Goals: _____

        _____

        _____

        _____

        _____

Summary

In this chapter I have presented techniques for Goal Setting. The three key points were:

    1. Set goals that are directly under your control.

2. Base your goals on actions that you can take that should lead to a reduction of your fear-provoking thoughts.

3. Be specific, so that if you achieve your goal, but the consequence you hoped it would bring about does not occur, you can still recognize that you have been successful in attaining your goal.

7

DEALING WITH AVOIDANCE
AND PROCRASTINATION

In this chapter I will explain how avoidance is used to reduce stage-fright and why its effects are so powerful, explain how procrastination has a similar but sometimes more harmful result, and present Stress Inoculation techniques for dealing with avoidance and procrastination.

Avoidance

One of the most popular methods of reducing stagefright is *not performing*—avoiding it altogether. The problem with avoidance is that it makes you feel better in the short run, but worse in the long run. Avoidance succeeds in reducing the anxiety you would face by appearing before an audience, but it does not help the bad feelings you develop when you pass up a better job, decline a nomination to an office in some organization, or lose an opportunity to assume a leadership role because it requires you to present your views to others. Self-esteem suffers greatly whenever *your fears control you* rather than *you controlling your fears*.

Avoidance feeds on itself! When you avoid something and get rewarded for it, avoidance is reinforced. You're more likely to avoid again next time. Here is an example of how avoidance gets rewarded . . . at first:

The Case of Rod R. (Cont.)

Rod R. was an attorney who came to me initially because he was afraid to appear in court. It turned out that he was also very shy and afraid to approach women and begin a conversation. Each time he would try to approach a woman, he would begin to think of what he would say to her, and then imagine her reaction—which was always a rejection! These thoughts made his anxiety level rise very quickly. To calm himself, he would turn away to avoid the woman. This would immediately calm him—but he was a very lonely guy!

I mentioned earlier that public speaking phobia is the number one fear in America. The reason so many people choose to avoid public speaking is that *avoidance works*. It *immediately* reduces the fear. Unfortunately, each time it works, the habit of avoidance gets a little stronger, and the rewards to be gained by giving such talks are lost. Whenever anyone with a phobia comes to me, the first question I ask is always, "How long have you had this fear?" The longer the fear has lasted, the more it has probably been avoided, and the longer it will probably take to lose.

Approach-Avoidance Conflicts

Typically, avoidance is a choice made to resolve a conflict. Of all the conflicts that psychologists have studied, approach-avoidance conflicts are about the most difficult to treat. They occur whenever you have to make a choice that involves both positive and negative elements: where you *cannot have one without the other*. For example, if we look further at the case of Rod R., he was constantly in approach-avoidance conflict situations with women. He wanted to talk to them (approach), but he was afraid of the rejection and anxiety (avoidance). He had stagefright with an audience of one.

In approach-avoidance conflicts, the tendency to avoid is almost always stronger than the tendency to approach. This leads to an interesting problem: *Quite often the rewards for performing are obscured by fear-provoking thoughts and their accompanying anxiety.* One way to solve this problem and overcome avoidance is to identify and focus on the rewards for successfully performing.

Practice Exercise 12:
Identifying the Rewards for Performing and Avoiding

Think of a performance task that you have been avoiding, such as public speaking, taking an interview, or asking someone for a date. Make a list of the benefits you would receive if you actually did it. Make sure you identify both the long- and short-term benefits.

Once you have identified the benefits of performing, do the same thing for the benefits of avoiding that task. See what rewards you get from *not* doing that task.

Rewards for Performing	Rewards for Avoiding

Here is an example of how the exercise should be done. I will use asking someone out for a date as the task (notice that I am discussing the act of asking someone for a date, not actually getting the date):

Rewards for Performing	Rewards for Avoiding
1. *Feel proud of myself for having the courage to do something difficult.*	1. *Not experiencing rejection, and endangering self-esteem.*
2. *Increasing the likelihood of going on a date and enjoying myself.*	2. *Lowering anxiety by knowing that I will not have to deal with the confrontation or rejection.*
3. *Increasing the likelihood of finding a lifetime partner.*	

4. *Increasing my social skills,*
   which make each successive
   encounter more likely to succeed.

You must learn to keep the rewards for performing in mind to help you overcome the tendency to avoid. As you get anxious, there is a strong tendency to dwell on your fear-provoking thoughts and forget the possible rewards to be gained by your performance. As you focus your attention on the positive aspects of how you will present yourself to your audience, and what benefits may occur as a result of it, you will weaken the tendency to avoid.

Procrastination

Sometimes you will find yourself forced into a position where you must perform. Even here you can *almost avoid* by procrastinating. Procrastination is a nice word for stalling or putting things off. Although procrastination is similar to avoidance, it differs in one major way: when you finally do perform, it actually makes the performance worse. This is because it interferes with adequate preparation.

The Case of Gerald M.

Gerald M. was a graduate student at a local university who was enrolled in a seminar class. In a seminar class, each graduate student is expected to select a research area and thoroughly investigate it. He or she must then present the results of his or her investigation to the class in a talk that typically lasts for at least one hour. The graduate student giving the talk also must be prepared to answer a series of questions from other graduate students in the class, and from the professor. He or she is expected to have become an expert on the topic.

Gerald, like many students, found this situation very intimidating. He could not avoid it, however, if he wanted to earn his Master's Degree. Each time he thought about presenting his topic he got very tense. To calm himself, he put off preparing his speech—out of sight, out of mind!

Unfortunately for Gerald, when the time came for him to present his seminar paper, this led to a great deal of anxiety and a terrible speech. By putting it off he had less time to prepare, and therefore did a poor job.

The Con List

Whenever you have to make a crucial decision, such as performing or avoiding, you engage in an internal dialogue about it. You identify the *pro* and *con* arguments, and at the end of the dialogue, you either do it or not. From now on, *you will either do it, or else write down your best reasons for not doing it.*

Listening in on your own internal dialogues is a little like watching the old Saturday morning cartoons when you were a child. There was often a situation in which a character had to make a difficult moral choice. Out of nowhere, a little devil and angel would appear on his shoulders, and begin a dialogue. Eventually, one side or the other would win. This is remarkably close to your own situation.

In the following exercise you will identify the reasons you use to avoid and procrastinate—your **con** list. There are two important reasons for writing down these *con* arguments:

1. If you claim that you are not really avoiding, but only postponing, this argument will wear thin very quickly. After you notice yourself using it for the third or fourth time, you should actually blush from embarrassment each time you use it to avoid doing something.

2. In writing down your reasons, you will give yourself the opportunity to observe your actual reasoning processes more closely, and perhaps see some flaws in your arguments.

Practice Exercise 13: Preparing a Con List

This exercise will be most valuable to you if you are currently putting off work on an actual presentation. If you are not, then select any task that you have been putting off, such as exercising or dieting.

1. Each time you recognize that you have the opportunity to work on it but do not, write down the reason why.

2. Each time you put it off again, read the list before putting down your reasons. You will be surprised to see how difficult it is to use a reason after you have used it a few times already. Imagine how difficult it will be to say, "I'll just watch TV for a few minutes, and then I'll begin" when you have used it three or four times already and never began working.

Stress Inoculation

When you get a vaccination against a disease, you are actually getting a small dose of the disorder you hope to avoid. You will build up antibodies against the disease to protect you from it. Stress inoculation works on the same principle. You immerse yourself in a fear-provoking situation gradually, and adapt to it with repeated exposures. It works as if your body were building *anxiety antibodies*.

The way stress inoculation works is that the more closely you simulate the actual conditions of performing during practice, the more secure you will feel when it is time to perform. If you learn a skill in a safe, calm environment, and always practice within that safe environment, it will be very difficult for you to perform that particular skill when things are tense or dangerous.

An experiment performed during World War II showed that over 80 percent of the soldiers tested never fired their weapons in combat. In a slightly less dramatic example, a friend experienced a similar result.

The Case of George M.

George M. was a psychologist and outdoorsman. He learned to do an Eskimo roll in a kayak (i.e., righting yourself when the boat capsizes). This skill was acquired while training in a large swimming pool. When his kayak capsized in rough river rapids, he was unable to perform this maneuver. But he did survive.

Similarly, relaxation skills are usually learned and practiced in very safe environments, and are frequently ineffective under stress because they were never practiced under stressful conditions.

There are three major forms of stress inoculation used by psychologists. I will mention them by name so that if you or your friends are being treated by a psychologist you can compare notes, and sound like experts:

1. Systematic Desensitization (The Gradual Approach): In this technique you sneak up on the fear in small steps so that you get used to it. If you were about to enter a swimming pool in which the water was at 70°, you would start with one toe and proceed in very slowly, or perhaps start in an 80° pool and work your way down to the 70° pool.

2. Flooding (Comparable Practice): In this method you confront your fear head on. You would dive right into the 70° pool.

3. Implosion (Going Beyond): In this method you begin with a more difficult task than you will eventually have to face, so that by the time you are ready to perform, it seems easy by comparison. In this case you would practice diving into a pool that was 60°.

I will present each of these techniques to you individually, and suggest a way that you may practice each of them. As an example, let's imagine that you had to present a talk to an audience of seventy-five people.

Systematic Desensitization (The Gradual Approach)

In using this technique you would go through the following steps:

1. Identify a list of actions you could take to reach your goal of talking before a group of seventy-five people. You would approach this goal very slowly, beginning with a task or situation that was very far removed from the final goal itself.

2. Use your relaxation skills to become very relaxed at the beginning.

3. Try the first step while remaining as relaxed as possible. If you get too tense, stop and get yourself to relax. When you feel better, try it again. The rationale behind this technique is that after you have tried each small step enough times you will get so used to it that you will no longer be afraid of it.

4. As you master each step, proceed to the next one until you arrive at your goal.

It is much easier to see how this procedure works with a concrete example. The steps below show a common version of this technique that I have used many times with people who get anxious when speaking before a large audience:

1. Present the talk into a cassette recorder. You will be surprised to find out how much pressure a cassette recorder will put on you as you practice your talk into it. When you do such practicing, however, you must make a commitment not to stop. Perform just as if you had a *real* audience. Using a cassette recorder has a few other advantages:

- It gives you excellent feedback on what your talk sounds like.

- It lets you play the tape back so that you can use it to learn the material better. You can turn tedious situations, such as being stuck in traffic jams or cleaning out the garage, into opportunities to become better prepared by listening to your tapes.

2. Try the talk out on a friend or two, or a kindly family member. The more your small "audience" resembles the intended audience, the better. Be sure to remember that you may bore family or friends with a talk that would be very interesting to your intended audience.

3. Try the talk out on a few colleagues. This gets you still closer to your future audience. If you are feeling brave, ask them for feedback. If you are feeling even braver, listen to their feedback.

4. If possible, try the talk out on a group very similar to your intended audience. Often there are organizations who are looking for cheap (i.e., free) speakers. Sometimes you may find similar groups in related organizations. Remember, the closer you can get to the actual situation of talking to those seventy-five people, the better.

5. Give the talk to the seventy-five people in the actual audience. The last step in systematic desensitization is always performing the actual goal.

Practice Exercise 14: Systematic Desensitization

Using the next time that you will have to speak before a large group, go through each of the four steps presented above. If your particular type of stagefright is not related to speaking in front of a large group of people, design your own series of four gradual steps toward whatever task you must confront. Write down each of the four steps you will use below:

1. _____

_____

2. _____

3. _____

4. _____

Flooding (Comparable Practice)

This technique differs from the previous one in that you do not look for an easier version of the problem to begin with—*you begin with an identical one*. Using the previous example, you would begin with step five, giving the talk in front of the group of seventy-five people. This is obviously a much quicker procedure, but usually taken only by people who are very motivated or brave. The term *flooding* came about from the technique's use in overcoming water phobias. Instead of gradually acclimating people to water, you toss them right into it.

Implosion (Going Beyond)

If you had to give a talk in front of seventy-five people, using implosion you would begin by talking to an even larger group. The idea behind implosion is to go so far beyond what you have to do in your performance, that by the time you have practiced enough, the actual performance will seem like a trifle. Once I used this technique, although not intentionally.

The Case of Peter D.

Peter D. is a psychologist and very part-time musician. He was playing in a musical trio. They practiced weekly, and began to think they were getting pretty good. They decided to thrust themselves on an unsuspecting public by appearing at a few local nightclubs. Realizing that public appearances might make them nervous at first, and since one of their members was a clinical psychologist, it was decided that they would invite a few of their close friends to an intimate party and try out the act. This was to be an example of systematic desensitization, the gradual approach.

Soon, a few other friends heard about the party and asked to be invited. Within a week, there were over seventy-five "close" friends coming to the party. Somehow the trio survived that party, and began playing in clubs. Those clubs were nothing after the ordeal-by-fire of performing for seventy-five close friends.

High school basketball coaches frequently use implosion. Typically, their players train in a fairly quiet gym. They are used to hearing other players calling out to signal them, and they are used to hearing the sound of the basketball bouncing as they dribble. Then when they come to play their actual games, they are scared out of their wits by the noise and commotion of all the screaming fans. In using implosion, many coaches have their players practice with a very loud stereo playing. By the time they can play without being distracted by the loud music, a big crowd is easy to handle.

Summary

In this chapter I dealt with overcoming avoidance and procrastination. There are several important points to remember:

1. Avoidance is its own reward, because it reduces anxiety.

2. The intensity of anxiety often obscures the rewards for performing.

3. Procrastination is related to avoiding, but actually weakens a performance because it does not permit adequate preparation.

4. Stress inoculation techniques such as systematic desensitization, flooding, and implosion can be used effectively to deal with avoidance and procrastination.

8

IMPROVING MEMORY AND PERFORMANCE SKILLS

Many people are afraid that their memories will falter when they are in front of an audience. There are few things more frightening than standing before a group of people, who are giving you their undivided attention, and not knowing what you are about to say or do next. Such memory problems are actually very easy to attack.

Improving your memory relieves stagefright at the level of performance or direct action. Remembering the key points of your presentation instead of forgetting them is an obvious improvement in your performance. Seeing is believing—you see yourself performing better and take that as evidence to revise your negative thoughts and predictions. Here is an example:

The Case of Barbara G. (Revisited)

Barabra G., a chemist who was afraid of public speaking, was the first case study mentioned in this book. She was very afraid of forgetting information in her talk. I taught her a few memory improvement techniques *(change in performance)* to handle this problem. As she experienced an improvement in her memory during a speech, she began to believe that her memory was working better. This new appraisal of her memory led to a new prediction about her public speaking—that she would do better *(change in thought)*. This change in her prediction led to less anxiety *(change in emotion)*.

There are four basic ways to improve memory for a performance:

1. Reduce Anxiety

2. Reduce Self-Monitoring

3. Increase Organization

4. Practice

1. Reducing Anxiety

Since I dealt with directly reducing the symptoms of anxiety in the chapter on relaxation, I will only briefly mention the effect of anxiety on memory here. There have been many experiments demonstrating that high levels of anxiety worsen performance on memory tasks. Any student who has ever experienced *test anxiety* knows what happens to memory as anxiety is increased.

I performed a simple experiment to demonstrate the effects of social anxiety on short-term memory. University students in several of my seminar classes were asked to introduce themselves during the first class meeting. At the end of the round of introductions, the students were asked to write down the names of as many other students as they could remember. In almost every case, memory was worst for the students who sat on either side of them. This effect was clearly due to the *social anxiety* they experienced immediately before and after having to introduce themselves to the entire group.

So as the first step in improving your memory, do your relaxation exercises before each practice session and before your presentation.

2. Reducing Self-Monitoring

The brain is set up to handle only one difficult task at a time. This presents a major problem during a performance if you are experiencing butterflies. As you become self-conscious about your performance and yourself, you take your attention away from the performance and begin to examine yourself to see just how anxious you are. This is called *self-monitoring*.

Unfortunately, as you keep self-monitoring to see just how anxious you are, and just how badly you are doing, part of your attention is captured in this self-monitoring process. The more attention you give to self-monitoring, the less attention you have to give to your presentation. This will weaken your performance, which will make you more anxious, which will also weaken your performance—and the whole process just keeps going in a vicious cycle.

Before I show you how to control self-monitoring, I would like to demonstrate it so that you see how damaging its effects are to your performance of even a simple mental task.

Practice Exercise 15: The Effects of Self-Monitoring

Have a friend give you a telephone number (that you do not already know) to remember for just thirty seconds. During those thirty seconds I would like you to carry out the following self-monitoring task: Close your eyes and describe your physical appearance to your friend including the following things:

- *Your attire.* Make sure you include each article of your clothing, including its color and style, from the shoes up.

- *Your physical features.* Work from your face downward. Describe as many of your physical attributes as the time allows.

After the thirty seconds are up, try to repeat the telephone number to your friend. With any luck at all you will have forgotten most of it.

Techniques for Reducing Self-Monitoring

There are many ways to go about reducing your self-monitoring. A few of them are presented below:

1. Additional practice. One way to reduce the effects of self-monitoring is simply to become so good at whatever you are performing that increased self-monitoring will affect it less. There is good psychological evidence to show that the better you can do one task, the more you can perform another task simultaneously.

2. Attention focusing. One of the best methods for reducing or eliminating self-monitoring is to focus your attention back on the task you are supposed to be performing. If you are giving a talk and you notice yourself beginning to pay attention to your nervousness, there are several things you can do:

- Glance at your outline.

- Think of the next thing you are going to say.

- If a particular person is making you anxious, avoid looking at him or her.

3. Practice while self-monitoring. Most people get unnerved when they notice they have become distracted and have lost concentration. You can actually prepare for this by practicing your talk, *interrupting it with self-monitoring*, and then continuing with the talk. Practice starting and stopping your presentation so you can develop techniques for organization and retention. Many people practice in front of a mirror, and every so often look up as a distraction.

4. Monitoring the audience. Many times just seeing that a particular person is in the audience, or seeing someone who looks intimidating or bored, can be an enormous distraction. Here are two proven techniques for handling these situations:

- Avoid looking at them by staring out over the audience's heads. This gives the audience the illusion that you are actually looking at them, making eye contact—but little do they know.

- A personal favorite of mine is to imagine seeing the audience in their underwear. If someone seems to be particularly threatening or bothersome, imagine that the elastic on his underwear is stretched out. I have never been so frightened that I needed to imagine someone in dirty underwear, but if it helps you. . . .

3. Increasing Organization

The better organized something is, the easier it is to learn and remember. Since I teach courses that include the psychology of memory, here are a few examples taken from my classes to show you the relationship between organization and memory.

- **When there is organization already present.** There are many times when something you have to remember is already organized for you. This makes it easy for you, as long as you see the organization. Often people do not use organization because they do not know it is here. Look at the number below:

$$2\ 3\ 4\ 6\ 6\ 9\ 8$$

If you were asked to memorize it, how would you do it? Most of my students reorganize it. Some regroup it as follows: 234-6698, as if it were a telephone number. Others regroup it in three chunks: 234 - 66 - 98, because each grouping has a certain sort of meaning.

See what happens when you look at every other number to see a pattern:

$$2346698 = \begin{smallmatrix} 2 & 4 & 6 & 8 \\ & 3 & 6 & 9 \end{smallmatrix}$$

If you happened to see the organization here, it would not only help you to remember the order of the numbers, but also you could remember a number a mile long using the pattern that was established here.

Always examine any material you have to remember and present to determine its organization. The more the organization forms a pattern that may be meaningful to you, the better you can remember it.

- **When there is no apparent organization already present.** Sometimes what you see is what you get. If there is no organization, you can make up your own using mnemonic techniques (pronounced *neh-mon-ic*, the *m* is silent). These are memory devices or tricks. For example, children learning the names of the notes on the treble clef lines (EGBDF) use the following mnemonic: *Every good boy does fine.*

Practice Exercise 16: Using Mnemonic Techniques

I will give you a list of the planets in our solar system, in order of their distance from the sun. See how much of the list you can remember after reading it just *one* time. Then try it again using the mnemonic device I will provide for you. Here is the list:

**Mercury-Venus-Earth-Mars-
Jupiter-Saturn-Uranus-Neptune-Pluto**

Now cover it up and try to write it from memory.

Now try again using the mnemonic device below. Memorize the sentence, and use the first letter of each word to match up to the first letter in each planet name:

Man very easily makes jobs serve useful needs promptly

Write the name of each planet again, and see the difference.

Whenever you have to remember any sort of list, particularly in order, make up a mnemonic for remembering it. If you would like to go further in this area, read *The Memory Book* by Harry Lorayne and Jerry Lucas.

Now that you understand the role of organization in memory, here are a few techniques for increasing the organization of materials that you may be presenting:

Outlines. One of the easiest ways to increase the amount of organization in a presentation you plan to give is to outline it. Make sure the outline is functional for your talk. Write the outline so that it is easy to use for reference. Here are a few practical suggestions to make an outline more useful:

- The word or phrase should be written in a size that is large enough to be read easily. This is particularly important if the area where you have to make a presentation is not well lit.

- Color code key items to give them more instant recognition. You can use color coding to help instantly differentiate between various types of items on your outline such as concepts, explanations, and examples.

- In addition to just providing the organization of the presentation, the outline should contain *key words*. These can be used to cue stories and anecdotes as well as main points in the presentation.

Practice Exercise 17: Preparing an Outline

Using a talk that you are scheduled to give, or one that you know you will be called upon to give, prepare an outline for that talk. Your outline should have the following characteristics:

- It should reflect the conceptual organization of your topic, which will make the relation of any point to the overall topic clear.

- The outline should be easy to read and follow. To ensure this, try glancing away from it, then go back to it to find your place. If you cannot find it, you can be sure that it will be even worse under performance conditions.

- Color code the outline to differentiate concepts, examples, anecdotes, or any other types of entries.

- Indicate any *key words and phrases.*

Writing out the complete text. For those people who tend to panic, or who have found that they can end up completely lost or tongue-tied, here is a surefire technique to help you. Write out the complete text of your talk, and keep it with you when you give your presentation. You do not actually have to read it, but you will know it is there. This way you know that if worse comes to worst, you will be able to get through the presentation.

Practice Exercise 18: Preparing the Complete Text

Using the same topic you used in the previous exercise, write out the complete text of your talk, just as you would say it. There are several important factors to keep in mind if you decide to use this technique:

1. Write the talk conversationally, as you would say it. Do not use the more formal, written style.

2. Include an outline in the margin. Make sure it is very easy to read.

3. Practice giving the talk without reading it, but make sure you keep following the outline.

4. Practice reading the text. If you should happen to need to read it, you should be practiced in doing so. One of the secrets to reducing stagefright is to avoid surprises during a performance.

5. Start giving your talk without reading it, then stop talking and practice picking up where you left off, but this time by reading it. If you should have to begin reading, you will not panic about how and where to jump in, because you will be well practiced at it.

4. Practicing

There is an old saying, "For every psychologist there is an equal and opposite psychologist." By reputation, psychologists find very few "universally true" facts. One of the few that all of them agree on is that *practice helps learning and memory*. There are many aspects of practice to be considered. Below are a few of the more important ones:

Practice Frequently

Here is another old saying, "Repetition is the mother of retention." The important thing here is for you to practice the performance a lot. You will soon find that the more times you have explained a concept or told a story, the easier it becomes.

A good example of this is joke telling. Most people find that they stumble through a joke the first time they tell it. They may have trouble remembering the punchline in just the right way, or find that they leave out important details or trip over a phrase or two. After you have told that particular joke a few times, your ability to tell it changes greatly. You will find that whole phrases leap from your mouth easily, and you can add nuances where appropriate. As you practice a talk by actually saying it repeatedly, you will get used to certain phrases, examples, and so on.

Use Imagery To Simulate the Actual Presentation Environment

You should always practice *as if* you were in the situation itself. If you mess up part of it, do not go back and begin again. Continue right from that difficult spot. Practice transitions to get you out of rough spots. Do not make jokes or asides that you would not use in the actual presentation.

Practice Incidentals

Do not confine your practicing to the substantive part of your presentation. Practice *everything* that you will say. This includes announcements, jokes, and anecdotes.

Practice as You Will Perform

Try to simulate every aspect of your performance during practice. My colleague plays tennis with a friend who tries to knock the cover off the ball in practice, then freezes up and barely hits the ball during an actual match. He loses a lot! *Practice as if you were performing*. If you do not joke during a performance, do not joke during practice. If you use notes during the talk, practice with the notes.

Practice Exercise 19: Practice Presentations

Practice your presentation exactly as you plan to give it. Try to practice as much as you can. If there are some particularly difficult or confusing parts, spend more time practicing those. Use opportunities like being stuck in rush hour traffic jams as practice times for those difficult areas.

To help simulate the actual presentation conditions, try to do one of the following:

1. Videotape your talk.

2. Tape-record your talk, and replay it as often as you can.

3. Get friends or colleagues to listen to your talk.

Practicing Physical Skills

There are additional complications in practicing physical skills. These skills are learned in two ways:

1. Physical skills can be learned by guiding the performance through *thinking* about each skill as it is performed.

2. Physical skills can also be learned by *muscle memory*. When you perform a physical act like hitting a baseball or playing a sonata on the piano, you usually do not have to think about how to make your body move. This means you have learned it through muscle memory. You begin to understand how powerful muscle memory is when you try to alter it. Anyone who has taken golf or tennis lessons has experienced the power of muscle memory as they tried to correct a "comfortable" swing or stroke.

The problem with trying to perform physical skills under pressure is that most people do their practicing using muscle memory and then do not use it during the tense situations in performance. As you get progressively more tense, muscle memory is interfered with, and the movements no longer *feel* the same.

At this point, you will generally begin *thinking* about how to do it. This throws off the *natural feel* which is achieved by relying on muscle memory—as you practiced it. Under these conditions, many people may actually forget how to perform a physical skill, and panic.

Practice Exercise 20: Practicing Physical Skills

Take a physical skill that you will have to perform under stress and *practice it both ways*. Spend some time thinking about the skill as you do it, as well as just doing it. When you find yourself under tense conditions, you will have some familiarity with thinking about the skill, and performing it while thinking. Whenever possible, try to either put yourself into tense situations, or use imagery to approximate these conditions.

Summary

In this chapter I presented several alternative ways to improve memory, which included:

1. Reducing anxiety

2. Reducing self-monitoring

3. Increasing organization

4. Increased and improved practice

9

SHYNESS

So far I have emphasized mostly larger audiences, and only dealt with a few examples of an audience of one, usually in an interview situation. Here I will deal with the most frequent example of stagefright with an audience of one: shyness.

Like all forms of stagefright, shyness is brought about by predictions of unpleasant events or outcomes and the fear of negative evaluation. It is simply stagefright with an audience of one. Social psychologist Arnold Buss points out that the fear-provoking, negative thoughts of many shy people center around low self-esteem. In an excellent book on shyness, Phillip Zimbardo also reported that his research showed a very strong relationship between shyness and situations producing low self-esteem.

The Case of Stacey G.

Although Stacey came to me with a problem in public speaking, one day she blurted out an interesting lament. "How come the only men I ever attract are pushy, aggressive, and insensitive?" Very rarely were questions this easy to answer. In the two months that I had worked with Stacey, I don't think we made eye contact more than five or six times, and the few times we did, it was fleeting. While we worked, she would practically curl up into a ball on the chair. She would generally end up looking away from me while pulling her legs up under herself, grabbing her knees. For me, the most incongruous thing about seeing her like this was that she mentioned that she felt more comfortable talking to me than almost any man she had ever met.

Whether Stacey was at a party or a library her outward behavior was always the same. She stared downward, avoiding eye contact with anyone in the room. A young man who wanted to meet her and was waiting for the opportunity to have her meet his gaze so he could smile at her and see if she smiled back was in for a long night. What kind of men would be able to break through her carefully erected social wall? What kind of men didn't need the reassurance of a friendly smile or prolonged eye contact before they walked up and started talking to her? The only ones brave enough were pushy, aggressive, and insensitive men. They were the ones who were not afraid of rejection. They would be able to walk right through her defenses and confront her. Unfortunately, men who ranged from painfully shy to slightly above average social interactors never stood a chance with her. Ironically, Stacey would have been much more likely to have a good relationship with one of her shyer admirers.

This is not a rare, isolated case. Philip Zimbardo writes that 80 percent of the people responding to the Stanford Shyness Survey reported being shy at some point in their lives. Forty percent reported being presently shy. That comes down to four out of ten people, or approximately 84 million people in the U.S. Out of this 40 percent, 25 percent reported being chronically shy, and 4 percent claimed to be shy all the time. That adds up to a lot of feelings, thoughts, and observations that are never shared.

How Shyness Differs From Stagefright

Stagefright and shyness are closely related. Social and clinical psychologists class both problems under the general area of social anxiety or social phobia. Shyness differs from stagefright in that it occurs only in groups where there is give-and-take, or interaction. In the case of stagefright there is generally a performer and audience. There is very limited interaction, such as a question-and-answer period at the end of a speech. Evaluation plays a smaller role in shyness than it does in stagefright.

Stagefright is much more common than shyness. People, when given the choice of meeting a stranger or giving a talk in public, will almost always choose the stranger. Furthermore, almost all shy people experience stagefright, but only a fraction of the population that experience stagefright experience shyness. When you fear something and can avoid it, there is not much of a problem. Many people are able to avoid situations in which they have to perform in front of an audience. When the feared situation is common social interaction, a necessity in everyday life, the shy person finds that quality of life is seriously threatened. You can see why shyness can have more serious and frequent negative consequences than stagefright.

In a series of experiments, Arnold Buss and his colleagues showed that shyness was not related very strongly to sociability: the desire to be with people. Instead, it related very strongly to fearfulness as a character trait. Shy people like to be around other people, but they are afraid to interact with them.

Indications of Shyness

Shyness is defined by Buss as discomfort, inhibition, and awkwardness in social situations, particularly with people who are unfamiliar. Shyness is expressed in three ways:

Behaviorally. Shy people are defined more by what they don't do than by specific things that they do. They are withdrawn and inhibited about interacting with others. In groups, shy people stay on the fringe. They respond to others in the most minimal ways. When someone asks them a question, they speak softly, and may even mumble. When shyness is extreme, there are visible signs of anxiety, such as trembling hands.

Emotionally. Shy people have two main emotional reactions: fear and self-consciousness. If *fear* predominates, the sympathetic nervous system reacts with quickened heartbeat, elevated blood pressure, and sweating. If *self-consciousness* predominates, the parasympathetic nervous system causes blushing. The latter response is generally a milder form of shyness.

Cognitively. If fear predominates, the shy person may experience panic in the immediate present and worry about future social interactions. If self-consciousness predominates, he or she may feel naked and vulnerable. Worry about being inept and doing something wrong or embarrassing my take over.

Causes of Shyness

The greatest cause of shyness is *novelty*. Novelty comes from the presence of new people or new situations. As you enter new neighborhoods, new schools, new jobs, or meet new people, you probably tend to act more shy. As you assume new social roles, novelty greatly increases.

In children, the precursor to shyness is Stranger Anxiety. Real shyness seems to begin around the ages of four to five years. Probably the most intense time is when children reach adolescence and experience a period of constant change. Shyness is very prevalent in adolescents, more so in girls than boys. By adulthood, the gender difference disappears.

There are four major factors that seem to cause shyness:

1. A Fear of People

Shyness often manifests itself as a fear of people. As you can see from the results presented below, people retain a fear of strangers. These results are from a survey of college students taken by Zimbardo.

- 70 percent of the students felt shy around strangers.

- 68 percent of the students felt shy around members of the opposite sex.

- 55 percent of the students felt shy around authorities by virtue of their knowledge.

- 40 percent of the students felt shy around authorities by virtue of their roles.

Of particular note is the effect of authority figures. Because the fear of negative evaluation is so strong, and authorities are the best at identifying when someone does not perform adequately, it is no surprise that they elicit shyness so frequently.

2. Situations That Invoke a Fear of Negative Evaluation

Generally, as the formality of a situation increases, shyness increases with it. Graduations, funerals, weddings, and public events are examples of situations in which shyness is greatly intensified. There are two reasons why this happens:

- When there are many rules, and an insistence that they be followed, there is a greater likelihood of making mistakes. Saying the wrong thing to the widow, or giving the wrong kind of gifts, can lead to exposure and embarrassment.

- The more public the event, the more exposed and vulnerable you feel in the situation. As you mess up, there are many more people who will find out . . . in a hurry.

Situations in which there is a great deal of social attention cause shyness. If there is too much or too little, you may tend to feel shy. Being ignored at a party is just as difficult and embarrassing as suddenly having the spotlight placed on you. A breach of privacy is another cause of shyness. When the public/private barrier is lowered, shyness usually results. People suffer a great deal of embarrassment when they are observed doing something in private. The results from Zimbardo's survey of college students show how they reacted to shy-provoking situations:

- 73 percent of the students felt shy about giving a speech.

- 68 percent of the students felt shy about being around large groups of people.

- 55 percent of the students felt shy about being in social situations

- 55 percent of the students felt shy about being in new situations.

- 54 percent of the students felt shy about being in situations requiring assertiveness.

- 54 percent of the students felt shy about being in situations in which they were being evaluated.

3. Low Self-Esteem and Feelings of Unworthiness

The poorer your evaluation of yourself, the less willing you will be to interact with others. Your predictions about the outcomes of social interactions will tend to be negative. If you believe that you are ugly, you will be hesitant about asking someone out on a date. If you believe you are boring, you will avoid intimate dinner parties.

4. A Perceived Lack of Social Skills

The Case of Steve N.

Steve N. was brought up in a family in which lack of communication and intimacy was the rule. As a youngster he was a ham radio operator, and preferred the company of machines to other kids. At the age of forty-five, he had a wife and three children, and worked as an accountant. His wife raised the children with minimal input from him. He chose a profession that was solitary, and where his major interactions were with computers and numbers. His family complained that he never showed any emotion toward them. When things got difficult, he would leave the room and turn on his computer.

What got his family most frustrated was that he showed a great deal of affection toward the family dog, but was unable to show them any emotion at all. Within our first session, he stated very clearly that he felt so awkward in social situations that it was easier to deal with the consequences of leaving the room than looking awkward and being embarrassed. He had a major skill deficit. He avoided communication because he thought he would lose more by communicating badly than by not communicating at all. The last section of this chapter is devoted to the development of social skills.

Steve's own family background is consistent with research that showed that parents of thirty-month-old shy children were more inhibited than parents of uninhibited children.

Consequences of Shyness

If shyness is allowed to go unchecked, it often leads to loneliness and depression. Shy people tend to have fewer friends and less frequent romantic partners. In relationships, shy people will generally choose to hold back. They are not as free to divulge their feelings, their wants, and even their complaints. They prefer the security of not asking and not telling to the risk of taking a chance and getting hurt. More often than not, they tend to do nothing active in relationships for fear of putting themselves at risk. Shy people tend to get into relationships less often, and they also hold on to bad relationships longer to avoid confrontation and the risks involved with trying to find another relationship.

One long-term study followed individuals who were shy and reserved in late childhood and traced the continuities and consequences of this behavior over a thirty-year period of their lives. Shy boys were more likely to delay getting married, having children, and attaining a stable career. They achieved lower occupational achievement and stability, along with lower marital stability. Shy girls were more likely than their peers to follow a conventional pattern of marriage, childbearing, and homemaking.

Three social psychologists—Robert L. Montgomery, Francis M. Haemmerlie, and Mary Edwards—identified many debilitating effects of shyness on people's lives. Their research concluded that shy people consistently judged themselves to be less physically attractive. They had fewer friends and received less in the way of social support from each of their few friends. Yet another study showed a strong relationship between loneliness and shyness, and also found that shy people were less happy.

The Risks of Shyness

Shy people often consider their reactions inappropriate, so they prefer to be alone rather than to be embarrassed in public. They choose protective *isolation*. Unfortunately, shyness lowers attention in both social and work situations. The more self-preoccupied you are, the less attention you have available for the task at hand. This leads to poorer performance at work, and worse functioning in relationships. People in this situation help bring about their own fears.

Shyness often leads to *boredom*. Because they try to avoid interaction, shy people often develop a repetitive lifestyle that is based more on safety needs than on pleasure-seeking. Since shyness and fearfulness are so closely linked, shy people tend not to experiment with new events, activities, or new social circles.

Interestingly, shy people tend toward *narcissism*. They are preoccupied with themselves. They have many thoughts and fantasies that they never get to act on. Furthermore, although self-examination and self-analysis are generally signs of adaptive psychological functioning, in the shy person, it tends to become dysfunctionally obsessive. Eighty-five percent of the people who report being shy admit that they are excessively preoccupied with themselves.

Overcoming Shyness

The Case of Jim C.

Jim C. was a young attorney who believed that people thought of him as worthless. He believed that as soon as he approached someone, particularly a potential date, the person would recognize his worthlessness. The closer he came to approaching someone, the more he would frighten himself by thinking about how he would disgrace himself. Then he would think about how awkward and embarrassed he would become as a result of such a disgrace.

Aaron Beck and Gary Emory have pointed out that in cases of social anxiety, like shyness, the consequences of a poor interaction are almost always exaggerated. Jim C. believed that the first time he said something stupid he would be publicly humiliated. He believed that people would actually say they thought he was worthless, and laugh at him.

Interestingly, he appeared quiet and shy, while on the inside he was ablaze with fear and panic. If you are shy, you know that, although you appear quiet to others, your mind is generally going a mile-a-minute with fear-provoking thoughts.

The situational nature of shyness is very evident with Jim C. Although he was very shy around women, he was very outspoken in court. He was very confident with his clients and colleagues about professional matters. His opinion about his abilities as an attorney was quite high.

The basic formula for stagefright applies to shyness as well. You can predict how much shyness you will experience by looking at two factors: your prediction of how successfully you will perform and how important you think the consequences of your performance.

Practice Exercise 21: Identifying
Fear-Provoking Thoughts Leading to Shyness

As in dealing with all other forms of stagefright, the first step is identifying the fear-provoking thoughts that make you want to avoid social situations. Below are a few common fear-provoking thoughts leading to shyness. Put a check by the ones that sound familiar, and add your own thoughts at the end.

- ☐ I'm ugly.
- ☐ I don't know how to do anything well.
- ☐ I'm unlikable.
- ☐ I'll make a bad impression.
- ☐ I'm just not stylish or contemporary.
- ☐ I'm boring.
- ☐ I sound too negative and pessimistic.
- ☐ I'm not being sociable enough.
- ☐ I can't be intimate with people.
- ☐ I can't stand being the center of attention.
- ☐ I can't stand being compared to others.
- ☐ I'm hopeless dealing with the opposite sex.

Your own additional thoughts:

_____

_____

_____

_____

_____

Practice Exercise 22: Goal Setting

Now that you have an idea about how you have been thinking yourself into being shy, it is time to see what being shy has kept you from doing. Make a list of five things you would like to accomplish if your shyness did not keep you from achieving it. Express your goals in terms of actions you can take that are under your direct control:

1. _____

_____

2. _____

_____

3. _____

_____

4. _____

_____

5. _____

_____

Take the items in the list and arrange them from easy to hard in terms of what it would take to accomplish them. See the chapter on goal setting, which details information on how to achieve your goals.

Social Skills Training

All of the techniques for controlling stagefright discussed so far can be applied to overcoming shyness and reaching your goals. There is an additional approach that is presented in this section. Speech communication expert Lynne Kelly presents excellent evidence to support the use of social skills training as a way to control social anxiety. She points out that there are two different types of social skills training:

1. **Skill acquisition**. This is for people who have not learned certain essential social skills.

2. **Skill practice**. This is for people who have learned the skills, but need to practice them so they can be used effectively.

In my work with shy people, I have found it useful to make the same distinction between learning the skills and practicing them. I will begin with a group of very useful skill-learning exercises dealing with two areas in which people experience shyness: conversation and assertion. If you are not sure whether you need to learn these skills, read them over and you will easily determine if you need them.

Learning New Conversation Skills

The Case of Ron M.

For Ron M., one of the most awkward situations is when a group of people are engaged in a conversation that he wants to enter. He always feels that he draws too much attention to himself, and makes everyone involved feel uncomfortable. He says he never knows the right thing to say, and even if he did, he would not know the right time to say it.

I have met many people who dread going to parties for this very reason. The exercise below presents the steps involved.

Practice Exercise 23:
Entering Into a Conversation Group

In this skill there are three considerations:

1. Where you stand: When you first approach the group, stand a small step outside the circle of people. This leaves you in position to listen, but you're not conspicuously trying to become part of the group yet. Later, as you make your entering statement, you will be in position to take the small step required to take your position within the group.

2. What you say: Before attempting to enter the group, spend a short time listening to the conversation, both in terms of its content and tone. For example, it can cause you a great deal of embarrassment if you enter a conversation seriously when everyone else is joking. After you have listened for the conversation for a while, try rehearsing an appropriately interesting comment to use as your opening statement.

3. When you say it: When your statement is timely and relevant . . . make your move.

Whenever you have the opportunity to practice these skills, take it. Often people at work are engaged in conversations. Even though you may be comfortable enough with them to barge right in, don't.

Listen to them for a while, find the right opening, and then enter. Look for feedback from the group. If you improve, people will let you know by agreeing with what you say or complimenting you on your insightfulness.

You have probably noticed that some people are easy to talk to, while talking to other people can be a painful ordeal. Also, some people seem to have the ability to talk to anyone, but other people just seem to sit there awkwardly, not knowing what to say. There are definitely skills involved in making conversation.

Recently a colleague overheard this conversation at a party. A shy man was trying to get a conversation going with a woman who had just been introduced to him:

The Case of Jerry C.

Jerry: Are you having a nice time at the party?

Alice: Yes.

Jerry: Do you know many people here?

Alice: Yes.

Jerry: Did you come here straight from work?

Alice: No.

Jerry: Do you work close by here?

Alice: Yes.

Jerry C. had not mastered the skill of *asking open-ended questions.* He asked questions in such a way that each question would terminate the discussion. Meanwhile, the pressure was always on him to come up with more questions. What is worse, he found out surprisingly little about Alice from each of her answers.

Practice Exercise 24: Question Asking

This exercise will focus on two important conversation skills: asking open-ended questions and listening for free information.

Practice thinking of open-ended questions—questions that cannot be answered with a single-word answer. Instead of asking if Alice knew anyone at the party, Jerry could have asked her to name the people she knew there. Instead of asking if she worked close by, he could have asked what she did. Each of these questions might have opened Alice up, making it easier for Jerry to learn more about her.

This is an easy skill to practice because there are so many opportunities to practice it. Each time you are talking to someone, try to ask them some open-ended questions. Begin now by simply writing some practice questions to get the format clear:

_____

_____

_____

_____

_____

As you are asking these questions and listening to their answers, learn to listen for "free information." Free information refers to information that is given, but not asked for. Free information gives you many more opportunities to get to know someone, and gives excellent source material for asking new questions.

As you learn to appreciate others giving you free information, use that appreciation as motivation for you to give others free information as you talk. It makes it easier for other people to ask you questions. Furthermore, you can use this to steer conversations into areas that you would like to have discussed.

Another productive way to begin conversations is to give someone a compliment. You would think that giving and receiving compliments are two areas in which people certainly do not need help. Think about how many times you have heard someone else (because you would certainly never do this) respond to compliments this way:

Example I

Complimenter: You really gave a great talk yesterday.
Complimentee: It was no big deal . . . it was real ordinary.

Instead of graciously receiving the compliment, it was denied, and the complimenter's judgment was discounted.

Example 2

Complimenter: That's a great looking suit.
Complimentee: So's yours!

Here the attention is being diverted away from the compliment, and an obligatory compliment is being given in return. The return compliment feels very stiff and formal, and makes the other feel uncomfortable for having made the original compliment.

Practice Exercise 25:
Giving and Receiving Compliments

In this exercise begin your practice by giving people compliments. Here are a few factors that you should consider:

Selecting the compliment. Before you give people compliments, carefully identify what they have just done, and frame the compliments in a way they would like to hear them. A good way to practice this skill is to begin by complimenting strangers. Observe strangers and try to determine what type of compliment they would appreciate. For example, if they are dressed well, or are wearing a lot of jewelry, that is important to them. Thus, it would make good source material for a compliment. Chances are they would enjoy being noticed and complimented on their appearance.

Framing the compliment in short, descriptive terms. Avoid anything that would downgrade a compliment. For example, if you want to tell someone that you enjoyed their talk, say something like, "I really enjoyed your talk!" It sounds simple, doesn't it? Here are some common examples of how people abuse this "simple" principle:

"I'm terrible at giving speeches, but you did a great job." You tear yourself down as you give the compliment. Before anyone can enjoy the compliment you gave them, they have to build you up first: "Oh, no . . . you're real good too!"

"That was some speech." A compliment that is ambiguous, or even worse, sarcastic, is not a compliment at all.

"A lot of people seemed bored by your talk, I can't understand why, I thought it was great." This compliment is in the form of a mixed message. It is given with quite a bit of hostility.

Practice receiving compliments by offering polite thanks and appreciation. Many people believe that if they accept compliments, others will view them as acting arrogantly. They believe they must show modesty and a little protestation. If someone says you gave a great talk, you do not have to say, "Yes I was great ... as I always am!" There is a middle ground that permits you to say, "Thank you, that's great to hear. I've been preparing that talk for the past three weeks."

Learning Assertion Skills—How To Say "No"

Many people believe that it is better to do something you do not want than to have people dislike you. For them, saying no is not worth the guilt and alienation it will cause.

Practice Exercise 26: Saying "No"

Manual Smith wrote a wonderful book in 1975 on assertion training called *When I say No I Feel Guilty*. Almost any good book on assertion training will cover this topic, so I will only include a few basic principles here. There are four basic concerns when refusing a request. Each time you practice saying "no," make sure you consider each one:

1. Determine if the request is reasonable. Obviously, if it is not, do not agree to do it. Often, if you find yourself hesitating or questioning, it is a cue that it is not a reasonable request.

2. Clarify any aspects of the request that do not seem to be totally clear, and seek additional pertinent information if necessary. Often you would not agree to do something if you knew all the facts. Isn't that a good reason to get all the facts? The last two points could easily be referred to as "saying no with dignity."

3. Avoid excuses for saying no. Avoid making up reasons (lies) about why you "can't" comply with someone's request. If someone asks you to help him or her move, you do not have to say that you are ill or are having company that day.

4. Avoid apologizing when you say no. Apologizing weakens your position for refusing a request. By apologizing, you are saying you really believe that you should be agreeing.

Practicing Skills You Already Have

There are many times when you may have the necessary skills to do something but you do not use them. This usually occurs because you haven't practiced a skill enough to feel confident of the outcome.

Most skills must be practiced if they are to remain effective. At first they should be practiced in an environment that is as non-threatening as possible. If your ultimate wish is to meet new people and begin dating, do not begin practicing conversational skills on potential dating partners. Begin with people who will be safer. As you see your skill level begin increasing, then move closer to the type of people you want to date.

Practice Exercise 27:
Selecting Appropriate Practice Opportunities

Make a list of locations where you can practice your new skills safely:

_____

_____

_____

_____

_____

For example, it can be on line at the supermarket, or on line at the bank. Lines are a great place to start conversations because nobody enjoys standing and waiting, and you can always easily begin by getting others to join you in complaining about the situation.

Set a goal of how many times per day you will deliberately set out to practice your skills.

Practice Exercise 28:
Preparing a Dialogue in Advance

Quite often the stress of being in a new social situation can feel overwhelming. It will be much easier to cope with if you have some dialogue prepared in advance. You can do this by paying attention to current events, learning a few new (funny) jokes, or preparing a little lecture on the more interesting aspects of your work or hobby.

Also, prepare a list of conversation-starting remarks. There are a number of sources for these. Try to think of your own (this is a lot easier when you are not under stress), ask friends for the remarks they use, see what others use on you, or—if you are desperate enough—watch television and see what your favorite stars use.

Summary

In this chapter I have shown that shyness is related to stagefright. It is less common than stagefright, but can have greater everyday consequences. Shyness often develops from stranger anxiety, and involves a fear of negative evaluation and a sense of unworthiness. The consequences of living with shyness include isolation, depression, and impaired functioning both on the job and in social situations. Like stagefright, shyness depends on your predictions about how you will appear and the probable consequences of making a poor showing. All the techniques suggested for countering stagefright are appropriate for shyness. In addition, I presented special exercises for acquiring and practicing the social skills of entering a conversation, asking questions, giving and receiving compliments, and saying no.

10

PUBLIC SPEAKING TECHNIQUES

As I mentioned in the first chapter, public speaking phobia is the number one fear in America today. In this chapter I will cover some of the key techniques you should employ if you are going to do any public speaking.

In the tradition of Hollywood, I will break the chapter into three sequential areas:

1. **Pre-Production.** These are factors that go into the preparation of your talk.

2. **Production.** These are factors that go into giving the actual talk.

3. **Post-Production.** These are factors that should be considered after the talk has been given.

Pre-Production

1. Choosing a Topic

In many cases you will not have to worry about choosing a topic because one will already have been chosen for you. Most people who engage in public speaking are generally asked to do it, usually because of their *experience* and *expertise*. Should you find that you are ever called on to speak in public, and are given the opportunity to select your own topic, the two key words in the previous sentence should guide you in making a wise choice. Select a topic in which you have expertise and experience. It is always easier to give a talk when you know more than the audience.

2. Determining a Purpose

There are two basic reasons to give a talk in public: to inform and to entertain. It is not only possible, but essential to try to do both. In a good talk, the audience should walk away with some new information or skills that they can use in their daily lives, or at least as a discussion topic to make them more interesting at parties.

One of the things you should always keep in mind is the question, "What are the differences between print and speech?" If you merely want to inform an audience, why not just pass out a pamphlet? Your talk should utilize those factors that transcend print:

- Intonation
- Facial expressions
- Dialects
- Non-verbal techniques and gestures
- Eye contact and personal interaction

3. Establishing Your Credibility

Audiences will always show you more respect once they believe in your authenticity. Whether you have to write it into someone else's introduction of you, or into your speech, make sure you can present some convincing credentials. Include degrees, jobs held, people you have served, or honors you have earned.

4. Preparing the Material To Be Included

If you are already an expert on the topic, your biggest problem will probably not be finding enough to talk about, but rather limiting the material so that you can ram it into the time allotted to you. The most important considerations you will have to keep in mind are listed here:

Relate the talk to audience's perspective. Remember that your overall objectives are to inform and entertain. Let these two considerations guide your selection of material to be included. Never sacrifice information for the sake of entertainment, but if there is a choice between two pieces of information and one of them is more entertaining than the other—there is really no choice!

Whenever you can, select information or examples that will surprise the audience. If you can, select things that get them involved such as demonstrations, questions, or exercises they can participate in.

Limit the scope. Make sure you develop a tight outline in which each idea relates to the overall purpose of your talk. It is essential to avoid rambling.

Keep a tape recorder or pad with you at all times. Whenever you get an idea for something clever to include in your presentation, make sure you can record that idea immediately. It would be wonderful if all the good ideas came when you sat down to organize your talk with pad and pencil. Unfortunately, the good ideas are just as likely to come in a restaurant, on the freeway, or while standing in line at the bank. I literally keep making notes until my name is called to speak.

Use brainstorming. It is always a good idea to begin by just free associating on a pad or into a tape recorder, getting as many ideas for your talk as possible. If you have some friends who will help, that is even better. The key concept in brainstorming is quantity, not quality. The more ideas you can generate, the better. It is always easier to eliminate bad ideas later than it is to come up with ideas once you get stuck.

5. Researching the Topic

Find appropriate examples. Good examples that your audience can relate to are the key to effective presentations. They explain and broaden your concepts. They give them life and color.

Increase imagery. Always try to find examples that are lifelike and easy to imagine. The more the audience can make an empathic connection with your examples, the better they will receive your talk.

6. Visual Aids

When visual aids are appropriate, they do much to liven up a presentation. But be careful not to have them distract from your presentation.

7. Organizing the Talk

It has been said that most talks consist of a beginning, a *muddle*, and an end. Be careful!

Introduction. The introduction should let the audience know what they will hear. It also gives them their initial exposure to you. You must decide how you are to be viewed by them. Make sure that you get their attention in a way you want.

Your introduction should contain the basic outline of your presentation. This is particularly important if your talk is largely designed to inform the audience. The clearer the structure of your talk, the more of it the audience will follow and remember.

Body. As our little joke stated, be careful that the body of your talk is the middle, not the muddle. It is in the body of your presentation that you must limit the length of the presentation. Please remember the old saying, "nice guys finish fast!" Select only the information that is really essential. Too much detail makes a talk very tedious. Make your examples clear, and personalize them wherever possible.

Conclusion. In your conclusion, summarize or repeat all of the key points that you want the audience to walk away with. It is also the place where you will ask them to do something, if it is appropriate.

8. Editing the Talk

Shorten your presentation for greater effectiveness. There is almost never a reason to run over the time you have been given. It is certainly always better to leave your audience wanting more. Most talks are given a time limit for a reason. Whether it is a class (which will interfere with students' next class if you run over), or a panel (in which case you will usurp the next speaker's time), or simply a dinner where the organizers only wanted a short bit of entertainment— do not take more than your allotted time.

Double-space the initial draft. This way you can make easy editorial revisions. Very few great presentations are completed on the very first draft. Walk away from your first draft. Later, reread it and reflect on it. You will invariably see improvements you can make.

Write out the original version. Many people prefer to write out the original draft exactly as they intend to say it. Later they will use this as the basis of the outline they will actually use. Writing it out gives you the opportunity to time it and learn it.

As you edit the talk, make sure you use conversational language that will make your presentation easy to deliver and easy to understand.

9. Audience Involvement

Do whatever you can to involve the audience where this is appropriate. Below are a few suggestions to help you.

Ask questions. Ask the audience questions that you know they cannot answer, or that make them ponder the situation you present. If you can present an important question that they cannot answer, then they must turn to you, the expert. Furthermore, if your question is interesting to them, you will increase their attention level. If you can actually surprise or trick them with your answer, you will have them!

You can ask audience members to respond by yelling out the answer, telling the person seated next to them, raising a hand, or voting. All of this serves to increase their involvement in your talk.

Ask for comments. Many speakers solicit comments from their audience and then use the comments to launch into other areas. This is a particularly useful technique when you are very knowledgeable about your topic. It guarantees that your talk will be relevant to your audience.

Get them to ask you questions. You have all seen speakers ask the audience for questions. Some prefer questions as they go along, while others like to take the questions at the end. You should do whatever makes you feel more comfortable. If taking questions during the talk will throw you off, or keep you from structuring the talk the way you want, do not be afraid to limit questions to the end.

10. Advice

In many cases you will know how to prepare for a performance, but surely there will be times when you will not. In these cases, make use of colleagues or anyone who has more expertise or experience than you. Such people can be utilized in several ways:

To reduce uncertainty about what will happen. If you are worried about a particular audience's characteristics, find someone who has faced them before. They can provide you with both a description and advice.

To suggest preparation activities. People with experience can suggest ways for you to prepare that they have discovered. This advice would be very difficult to research or discover on your own.

To give you critiques on your performance. If you can get them to view your performance, they can be an excellent source of criticism and advice.

They can be used as role models. Observe good performers and emulate their performance wherever possible.

Production

11. Handouts

If there is a lot to remember, give the audience a handout to take with them. There is rarely a reason to make an audience take notes furiously to keep up with the information you are delivering. If there is a great deal of information, present an outline with blank lines between each item so that the audience can take notes right on it. If there is information that they will all surely want to write down, such as definitions, include the definitions right on the outline.

12. Non-Verbal Communication

Do not talk about things that make you uncomfortable. Audiences are very good at detecting when you are uncomfortable about a topic, joke, or example. If you are in doubt about whether to include it ... DON'T! This goes double if the material may possibly be in bad taste. The careers of Al Campanis, Jimmy the Greek, and Earl Butz would have been much brighter if they had heeded this advice.

Appear to enjoy giving the talk. You do not have to have a good time while you are giving your talk as long as you look like you are having a good time. The audience does not know if you are nervous as long as you are smiling, not messing up very badly, and not telling them that you're nervous.

Make eye contact. Eye contact is very important. It makes you appear more comfortable. It gives you feedback because you can see how the audience appears. For example, if you are getting quizzical looks from the audience, you may want to slow down or solicit questions.

13. Never, Never Apologize

Very often an audience thinks you are doing well, even though inside you are in extreme turmoil. Only a foolish speaker lets the audience know how he or she really feels. If you are nervous and you tell the audience, they believe you and begin trying to find evidence to support your claim. They will look at your hands more closely to see if they are trembling, and look to see if you are not making enough eye contact or are swallowing too much. Normally, they would not be trying to notice these things—unless you call their attention to them. DO NOT DO THIS!

14. Compliment the Audience and Show Them Respect

Poor speakers sometimes tell jokes, fail to get laughs, and then insult the audience for not getting the joke. Then the audience wants to kill them. Audiences, like most people, enjoy getting compliments. Give them some! If they belong to a prestigious group, praise them. If they share some outstanding trait, acknowledge it. If you cannot find some built-in audience trait on which they can be complimented, manufacture one. Tell them how attentive, well-informed, and clever they are. A corollary to this rule is to be humble. Never brag! Audiences rarely enjoy hearing anyone brag.

Post-Production

15. Evaluate the Talk

Now that you have given the talk, examine it and see what improvements you can make in it for next time. If there is a formal structure for feedback in place, such as written evaluation forms, grab them. If they do not exist, get as much feedback from participants as you can. You can always go to the person who invited you to give the presentation and ask if you provided what was needed. Usually people will come up to you and give you feedback. But if none do, try to get into conversations and solicit any information you can get.

Using Humor in Public Speaking

Humor is such a powerful tool for getting your point across that I have given humor its own section in this chapter.

Using humor to reduce anxiety is one of the best ways you can employ humor in your presentation. All of us have sat in a tense movie and seen the effects of comic relief. Humor gives us a respite from painful emotions. Here are two examples:

Example 1: *The Rhythm and Blues Singer*

A moderately well-known blind singer was led onto the stage. Before the audience could begin feeling sorry for him because of his handicap, he grabbed the microphone and said, "How are you all doing tonight? I'm outa' sight!" While the audience was laughing at this, he quickly added, "The reason I'm feeling so good is that I just got a great new lawyer. This guy has so much clout . . . he just got me a driver's license."

The audience saw how well-adjusted this singer was to his situation, and they were able to sit back and enjoy the show.

Example 2: *The Wheelchair*

I teach a class called Instructional Humor. The course is designed for people who are involved in public speaking and want to learn how to use humor to get their points across. One of the students in the class was a paraplegic psychotherapist. He said that when he gave talks he used to have trouble using humor because people felt so sorry for him. So he learned to begin his talks as follows: "Hi, it's always a pleasure to address a PRE-HANDICAPPED audience." It made the audience laugh and think. Before they could recover, he said, "I've got a new hobby: Chinese cooking. The other day I went into a utensil store and a woman came up and asked if she could help me. I said, 'sure . . . I wanna' wok.'"

Delivering Bad News

Humor has always been considered a good way to deliver bad news to people. Here are a few of the standard bad news delivery jokes to give you a feel for what I am talking about:

An avid golfer goes to a spiritual medium to try to contact his deceased golf partner. He succeeds and asks, "Jimmy, is there golf in heaven?"

His friend answers: "Mike, I have some good news and some bad news for you. The good news is, yes, there is golf and the playing conditions here are always perfect. The bad news is you're teeing off at 9:15 tomorrow morning.

* * *

A secretary told her boss that she had some good news and some bad news for him. He said, "Please, I've had such a bad day, I just couldn't stand any more bad news. Just give me the good news."

She said, "All right. . . . You're not sterile!"

* * *

A doctor told his patient, "I have some bad news and some worse news for you. The bad news is that you only have twenty-four hours to live."

His patient said, "What could possibly be worse news than that?"

The doctor said, "I tried to call you yesterday."

Avoid Hostile Humor

According to Sigmund Freud, most jokes that actually get laughs are rooted in hostility. Humor can be just another way of attacking people. For that reason, you should be very careful to determine whether you are attacking someone inadvertently when you tell a joke. The butt of the joke will surely recognize it even if you do not. Here is an obvious example of a hostile joke, using me as the butt:

Q: Why did Mrs. Desberg name her son Peter?

A: Because she couldn't spell blechhhh!

Remember all of the people who have gotten into trouble by telling hostile jokes, and remember the basic rule: If you don't say it, they can't repeat it, and you can't get into trouble! The rule you want to keep in mind is: DO NOT DIRECT HOSTILE JOKES AGAINST

YOUR AUDIENCE, OR TOWARD ANY GROUP WHERE YOU
COULD BE VIEWED AS DISCRIMINATORY.

The Case of George M. (Revisited)

George M. gave a talk at a psychological convention, and used
an old joke by Dorothy Parker, the famous Algonquin Roundtable wit.
Dorothy Parker had been asked to use the word *horticulture* in a sentence, and she said, "You can lead a *horticulture* . . . but you can't make
her think." The women in the audience actually booed him, and gave
him a hostile reception during the rest of his talk.

With these cautionary remarks in mind, here are a few more
examples of hostile jokes to give you a feel for them. Notice that they
can be very funny and effective—but only if used appropriately:

I asked a colleague, who was familiar with my work, what
I could do to improve my teaching skills. He said, "First
you should relax a little more . . . then you should stop
teaching for six months . . . then give it up!"

* * *

(A wife reading to her husband): "Your fortune says, 'you
are handsome, debonair, and wealthy' . . . "look, it even
has your weight wrong."

* * *

Two women approached a golf pro at a city golf course. He
turns to the first one and says, "Do you want to learn to
play golf?"

She says, "Oh no, it's my friend here who wants to learn. . . . I
learned yesterday!"

* * *

Q: What's the definition of tragedy?
A: A busload of lawyers going over a cliff . . . with two empty
   seats.

* * *

A consultant is someone who borrows your watch to tell
you what time it is . . . and then walks away with the
watch.

* * *

A consultant doesn't know any more than you do. She's just better organized and has slides.

* * *

Consultants are mystical people who ask a company for a number, and then give it back to them.

Consider using self-effacing humor to make yourself more accessible. You endear yourself to an audience when you tell jokes that make you the butt instead of the audience. This is a great way to get the power of hostile jokes without the worry about their effect. Here is a classic example told by Joan Rivers:

She said that she had been remodeling her home, and one day when she had an important appointment, her painter showed up late. He asked her what she wanted done, and she said, "Today I want you to paint the bedroom. I'm going for high drama and romance." With that she tore out a strand of her hair and said, "Paint the room the color of my hair!" That afternoon she returned to find that the walls were painted electric yellow and the ceiling was black.

Joke Delivery Techniques

Below are some techniques and tips for delivering jokes so that you can get their maximum benefit:

1. *Avoid jokes that are discriminatory or dirty.*

2. *Learn jokes before telling them.*

3. *Make use of the Rule of Three.* Basic jokes are structured by the Rule of Three. In the first part you establish a pattern. In the second part you confirm the pattern. In the third part you violate the pattern with a surprise. Here is an example:

Three men were commuting into New York City, having a discussion about which man's wife loved him the most.
The first man said, "My wife thinks I'm the most cultured man she ever met."

The second man said, "My wife thinks that I should have been an ambassador."

The third man said, "Your wives certainly sound like they're impressed with you, but mine brags about me all the time. Every time I stay home from work, and there's a knock at the door, my wife screams out . . . 'MY HUSBAND'S HOME!'"

4. *Always end the joke with the climactic word.* If you tell the punchline and there are a few more words coming after it, you will "step on your own laughs!"

5. *Don't laugh at your own jokes.* This is an obnoxious habit that seems to offend most audiences. Unless you are in character, and have a particular reason for laughing at your joke, avoid doing it.

6. *Don't repeat the punchline for a joke that works.* Some people think that if a joke happened to get a laugh, they can repeat the punchline and get more laughs. They will not.

7. *Don't explain jokes that don't work.* If you want to get an audience to really dislike you, all you have to do is tell them a joke that is not very funny. Then, when the audience does not laugh, assume that they did not get the joke, and explain it to them.

8. *Try to tell jokes or stories that can get laughs along the way to the punchline.* Here is an example:

An Englishman was visiting a New England fish cannery, and the supervisor was giving him a tour. He decided to show the conservative Britisher that Americans had a clever sense of humor. He pointed to a shelf of cans and said, "We eat all we can, and all we can't we can."

The Britisher just stared. Later that night he was having dinner with a friend and began chuckling. He said, "This American chap told me this frightfully amusing joke. We eat all we're able, and all we can't we tin."

Here are a few extra jokes you may find useful or—dare I suggest—amusing:

A new manager began by saying, "There are going to be a few changes in the system here. I'd like some input from

you. Those who oppose these changes may signify by
saying, 'I QUIT!'"

* * *

A good manager shouldn't get ulcers . . . he should give
them.

* * *

The better the news, the higher ranking the official who
announces it.

* * *

Retreat into analogies and discuss them until everyone has
forgotten the original problem.

* * *

To spot the expert, pick the one who predicts the job will
take the longest and cost the most.

* * *

A leader shouldn't get too far in front of his troops . . . or
he can get shot in the derriere.

* * *

People would rather live with a problem they cannot solve,
than a solution they don't understand.

* * *

A true friend will not laugh at your joke until she retells it!

* * *

There is no problem a good miracle cannot solve.

Humor can be a wonderful way to gain audience acceptance,
and I know that a fear of audience rejection is one of the most common fears leading to stagefright. Humor is particularly effective in an
environment where it is not expected. When you go to a comedy club
to hear comedians, the audience frequently has a tough attitude of
"Make me laugh!" In most cases, however, an audience is very grate-
ful for a chance to laugh. At the university, I find that students laugh
appreciatively because their expectation level for being entertained in
a classroom is so low.

My student evaluations are very highly correlated with the amount of humor I use. In most business situations, humor is even more appreciated.

Summary

In this chapter I have presented practical public speaking techniques for improving your preparation, actual presentation, and subsequent evaluation. A special section discussed the use of humor in public speaking.

11

INTERVIEWS AND AUDITIONS

In most interviews and auditions people actually sit and take notes right in front of you as you perform. Furthermore, the consequences of performing well in interviews and auditions are almost always important. You know that your presentation can have a major impact on your career and your future. There cannot be much more pressure in a performance situation. You may be convinced that friends at a party or neighbors at a PTA meeting are not really evaluating you, but here in an interview or audition . . . you are performing in front of people whose job it is to evaluate you!

This chapter will introduce you to various kinds of interviews and auditions. You'll find common interview questions and smart approaches to answering, as well as the sources of interview anxiety and how to beat them before your big day. You'll also find common audition pitfalls, and solutions suggested by seasoned performers. Fear of negative evaluation is the defining characteristic of stagefright—and the evaluation process is at its height during interviews and auditions. Knowing what you're in for is one key to success in an interview or audition. Another is creating the right frame of mind through investigative preparation and applied relaxation. You can conquer interview and audition anxiety as surely as you can conquer stagefright—and then reap the rewards of career advancement and professional success.

Interviews

Interviews obviously cause stress because the consequences are directly related to your survival. It is through the interview that you position yourself for future earnings and career advancement. Furthermore, you may believe that your opportunity for a certain type of interview is limited, and one particular interview may be a once-in-a-lifetime shot. That feeling can be strengthened if you got the interview through personal or family connections, or happened to be at the right place at the right time. It is important to know what you can expect so that you will not be caught unprepared, or be surprised by things you could have anticipated.

Types of Interviews

There are many different types of interviews, each with its own characteristics, requiring different types of preparation. Here are the most common ones:

Direct Interviews. Direct interviews are structured. This enables all candidates to be evaluated on the same criteria so that they may be compared to one another after all the interviews have been completed. The interviewer has a list of questions or an outline. Sometimes interviewers will use a formal checklist for scoring the candidates to facilitate comparisons. They may go so far as to use a point scoring system. Direct interviews are particularly common in selecting governmental positions ranging from civil service positions to hiring state university professors. This type of interview procedure highlights fairness. All candidates are supposed to get an even break.

Direct interviews offer less opportunity for the interviewers to get to know you well. You get limited opportunity to present the many facets of your personality. Because this type of interview suggests the interviewers have a lengthy list of candidates, your major goal here is to stand out positively in their minds when they review the results of all the interviews. Try to position yourself above the crowd.

Unstructured Interviews. Unstructured interviews usually get candidates to reveal as much information about themselves as possible. Questions tend to be broad and general. The goal is to discover as much about the candidate's personality as possible. This technique is generally used by non-professional interviewers. These interviews tend to be more informal. They offer an opportunity to get to know the candidate to see how well he or she will fit into the organization.

If you're at this stage, you don't need to emphasize your qualifications. The goal is to establish compatibility. The format may range from very supportive to stressful, but the goal remains the same: to determine if the candidate fits the spirit of the place. Be professional, but allow your personality to shine through. Ask yourself—and even the interviewer—whether the employer will be able to profit from your strengths.

Stress Interviews. Stress interviews use a combination of challenges, silence, and brusqueness to place the candidate under stress to see how he or she will handle the situation. An interview is rarely pure stress, and stress is often combined with unstructured interview formats. The key to performing well in this format is not to *show* stress, regardless of how much you are experiencing.

If a company uses a stress format, it is a good tip-off for you that the job will place you under considerable stress. Susan B. interviewed with a major transportation company and was stunned by how much pressure was placed on her during the interview. Transportation companies survive by doing things quickly, so stress is a major component in the industry. She got the job, and later discovered that almost all the key administrators were divorced, had ulcers, or were well on the road to alcoholism (in a few cases . . . all three).

Group Interviews. Group interviews have several interviewees and one or more interviewers. This format is cost-effective if there are many candidates to be interviewed. Its primary goal is to let certain characteristics of the candidates emerge from the interview. Generally, a group leader emerges, and shyness or unassertiveness is also accentuated.

Group interviews are very popular in the military, where the goal has been to identify those with leadership potential as rapidly as possible. One caution is that it is important to do background research on the characteristics of the employee that the company is looking for in this setting. In some cases, a company is looking for leaders, while in others it is looking for team players. In this case, the natural leader will be passed over in favor of the kind, supportive candidate.

Board Interviews. Board interviews have one candidate and a group of interviewers. These are common in situations such as graduate school oral defenses and interviews for important corporate positions. They tend to be very formal settings.

In a one-on-one interview, you try to establish rapport with the interviewer; this is obviously more difficult with a group of interviewers. The best thing you can do is to deal with the current question asked, and try to establish rapport during your response with the person who asked you that particular question.

Screening Interview. In large organizations, an initial level of interviewing is typically done by the Human Resources departments to determine the qualifications of the applicant. Their job is to filter out candidates that do not fulfill the basic job requisites. They look bad if they send an unqualified candidate forward and waste a manager's time, so they do not focus on personality variables. These are trained interviewers who try to determine if the candidate's resume is valid and whether there are inconsistencies. Their main goal is to weed out the unqualified applicants.

A screening interviewer has a list of the job specifications and must systematically determine if a candidate meets each of the requirements. The two keys to performing well on a screening interview follow:

1. Present the facts the interviewer is soliciting in the most direct, clear way possible. Do not volunteer anything that is not asked. You may volunteer something that is taken the wrong way, and takes you out of the running.

2. Maintain a pleasant, non-confrontational, non-controversial attitude.

Screeners cannot hire you; they can only reject you. Do not give them a reason for doing so. If you present yourself colorlessly but competently, you will move to the next round. If you seem like a qualified oddball, you will be rejected. The screening interviewer's main fear is facing a manager who yells, "How could you let a candidate like this through to the next level?"

Since screening interviewers are professionals whose main job is interviewing, the interview will proceed best if you let them lead. Do not attempt to shape or control the interview.

Selection Interview. Once you have gotten to a selection interview, your qualifications have been acknowledged. Now you are being looked at by your manager to see if he or she thinks you would be easy to work with. Your goal is to demonstrate your style and ability to fit in. The basic rule during selection interviews is to be the polite version of yourself. You do not want to pretend you are someone different for a number of reasons. The company may already have done some background research on you, including lengthy conversations with references. Now they want to see how you match that profile. Furthermore, you want them to know whom they are getting, to see if you will *both* be happy working together.

Because one of the goals is to determine your compatibility, stress may be introduced into the selection interview. If you are told something about which you want to disagree, do so in a courteous manner. First, you should acknowledge the validity of the others viewpoint. Then interject your own.

Six Common Mistakes During Interviews

Below are six common mistakes to avoid during the interview. Some are obvious, and some more subtle, but they all have the same thing in common. People have committed each of these mistakes, and not gotten hired.

1. Not dressing for the occasion, such as wearing unkempt clothes, or jeans where it would be appropriate to wear a suit and tie or a tailored dress. This is not the time or place to have an attitude. Appropriate dress shows appropriate courtesy and respect.

2. Showing up late. Arriving late for an interview is giving the interviewer a glimpse of sloppy work habits. The assumption he or she will make is likely to be: If he doesn't even show up on time to the interview, imagine when he will show up to work in the morning? Identify the time and place of the interview and make sure you will arrive well before that time, leaving room for any unforeseen events. If you're still late (which you mustn't be), apologize profusely.

3. Interrupting. Communication skills come under a magnifying glass during an interview. To interrupt is to broadcast: I am not a good listener. It also says that what you have to say is more important than what the interviewer has to say. This is a very poor way to make a good impression.

4. Using the interviewer's first name, or asking overly personal questions. This is equivalent to standing too close to someone you are talking to. It makes them uncomfortable, and shows disrespect.

5. Being inattentive. You must not permit your mind to wander. Pay attention to people's names, answer questions specifically, and so on. Your interviewers are judging you on how sharp you are.

6. Telling inappropriate jokes that are stereotyped and make fun of other groups based on gender, ethnicity, or whatever. Above all avoid obscene jokes. Many people use humor to diffuse tension, and it is a wonderful tool for doing so, *but only* if used appropriately. Telling the wrong joke can end the interview.

Strange But True Interview Stories

Vice presidents and personnel directors of the hundred largest corporations were asked to describe their most unusual experiences interviewing prospective employees. Here is a list of some memorable responses. Keep in mind that these are all true events:

- A job applicant challenged the interviewer to an arm wrestle.

- An interviewee wore a Walkman, explaining that she could listen to the interviewer and the music at the same time.

- A balding candidate excused himself and returned to the office a few minutes later wearing a hairpiece.

- An applicant said that if he was hired he would demonstrate his loyalty by having the corporate logo tattooed on his forearm.

- An applicant interrupted the interview to phone her therapist for advice on how to answer specific interview questions.

- A candidate brought a large dog to the interview.

- An applicant refused to sit down, and insisted on being interviewed standing up.

- A candidate dozed off during an interview.

Interview Preparation

One of the keys to interviewing effectively is to prepare before the interview. Your preparation shows your dedication and good work ethic. It shows the interviewer that you know how to research a topic, and that you do not do things in a superficial manner. Take a trip to your local library, and explore indexes to recent newspaper and magazine articles. Focus especially on publications that serve your particular industry. Also, don't hesitate to ask questions of your friends and colleagues in the field. At a minimum, you should determine the following information:

- *What does the company do?* You should know if they produce goods or provide services, or both.

- *Who are its major competitors,* and how does this company distinguish itself from the competition? This is essential because quite often you will be asked why you chose this company to work for.

- *What is the company's reputation is the marketplace?* This can be a sensitive issue. If any controversies are raging in the marketplace, you may be asked about them. You will look bad if you have never heard of the issues, and sharp if you can offer an informed opinion.

- *Is the company growing or downsizing?* You should be aware of the state of the industry. You may be asked for specific suggestions on how you would handle various aspects of growth or decline.

- *What are the major books, publications, and professional organizations in your field?* Knowing the titles and the issues shows your involvement in your profession. To show ignorance here shows that you are a dilettante or a dabbler rather than a serious professional. Be prepared to be asked if you are a member of any of these organizations or a subscriber to the publications.

- *What are the current trends, alternative points of view, and competing theories?* This is also a quick way for an interviewer to check out your dedication to your chosen field.

- *Identify job specifications before the interview.* Try to determine a hierarchical rating of precise qualities the interviewer is looking for. That way you can tailor your responses to fit the job better.

Also get yourself ready. **Dress appropriately for the interview.** There is a big difference between going to work in an artistic setting and in a corporate executive situation. In either case, do not wear anything extreme. I once read an interview with a Brooks Brothers salesman. Brooks Brothers is mecca for corporate executives when it comes to buying clothes. The salesman said that people do not come to Brooks Brothers because they like the look of the clothes. They shop there because they know that if they show up to an important meeting in a Brooks Brothers suit or dress, they cannot be wrong. It is a great example of dressing defensively. In Japan, the conservatively cut gray suit is almost like a uniform for executives. Similarly, aftershaves and perfumes should be minimal and understated.

It is the preparation that leads to success in an interview. There is an old expression in boxing: Fights are won and lost in the gym. A problem for many interviewees is that the interviewer will control the interview, asking the questions he or she wants answered. That doesn't mean you can't prepare. Remember that, since you are selling yourself, your job is to bring the interview around to your strengths.

Answering Questions

Interviews are simply structured. For the most part, they ask questions and you answer them! Still, you can influence the content of the interview by emphasizing your strengths. Make sure you listen to each question carefully. Assume there is a specific purpose behind each question, and answer it accordingly. To a perceptive interviewer, you are showing your ability to attend and carry out a talk to specifications—an important quality to a manager. If some aspect of the question is unclear, it is better to ask for clarification, or to present several ways of answering the question, rather than to assume you know ... and be way off. Getting clarification also gives you additional time to frame your response to the question. It is appropriate to take a few seconds before answering a question to think it over. Most interviewers will take this as a good sign. In most interviews, certain standard questions will come up. You will do well to have thought out a response in advance.

Seven Commonly Asked Questions

1. Tell me about yourself. It is much better to answer this question if you have done adequate preparation, and have an answer formulated. Generally, the interviewer is as interested in how you will handle such an open-ended question as in the content of your answer. Your style of responding here is very important. Don't ramble. Select three or four highlights of your strengths and abilities, and back each point up with an example or two from your past.

2. Explain any difficult circumstances at a previous job, and the conditions under which you left. If you had a personality clash with a former supervisor, or some other difficulty, there are several steps you must take:

- *Prepare for a reference check.* Most previous job sites are very cautious about giving out bad references, because they can be liable in court unless they have substantial documentation to back it up. One alternative you have, if there is a difficult or sensitive history at a company, is to have a friend do a sample reference check for you. Have your ally contact your previous place of employment as a potential employer, and determine what sort of information that company is giving out. That way, you can build your responses in line with the information the current interviewer will receive. If the reference is particularly negative, consider alternate references.

- *Frame the reason for leaving honestly, but in the best light for yourself.* Make sure your response is compatible with the reference check material. Since you are there, you can present the facts in the way that presents you best.

- *Accept responsibility for past problems.* You can complain about people you've had problems with in the past, as long as you also accept the responsibility for not having tried hard enough. Then, point out how you would handle the situation differently today. This shows the interviewer that you do not get defensive, can admit you are fallible, and you learn from your mistakes. Avoid telling bad stories about past job situations. It often backfires. Only do so if pressed hard. Then explain that you are only telling your side of the story.

- *If you are asked a question you do not wish to answer about the past, do not be evasive or cute.* Be specific about why you do not wish to answer it.

3. Why do you want to work in this field, or at this job? Here the goal of the interviewer is to discover your motivation. This question gives you an opportunity to present any anecdotes covering what drew you into this area. It also affords you the chance to identify specific talents or skills you wish the interviewer to note.

4. Why do you want to work for this specific company? This question affords you the opportunity to demonstrate your preparation and research. It is your chance to show that you have looked into this company, and why you believe it is a good fit for you.

5. What are your career objectives? This question reveals your level of aspiration. It also shows how long you intend to stay with the company. It's good to sound both ambitious and loyal.

6. What are your unique qualifications? Although this questions affords you the opportunity to brag about yourself, it is important that the response be framed in terms that do not sound like bragging. You want to sound self-confident without being too impressed with yourself.

7. What are your strengths and weaknesses? This is a very common question, and the difficult part is identifying weaknesses. You must find one or more good weaknesses to present. They cannot be too bad or extreme. A serious weakness is a sure way to lose a potential job. The basic rule here is to present a weakness with a plan for how you are dealing with it. It affords you another opportunity to show that you are fallible, but always looking to improve.

Additional Tips for Interview Success

Remember the interviewer's name. Ask for this name beforehand. You can do so on the phone when you set up the interview, or even get the name from the receptionist or secretary when you arrive. Chances are you'll feel stress during the beginning of the interview, particularly during the first two minutes, which is when introductions are being made. This is when the influences of novelty and stress are at their highest, and you have the *least* chance of remembering a name. If you cannot find out the name in advance, try to use the person's name right after it is told to you. For example, "Hi, Ms. Sanders." Do not use the interviewer's first name unless asked to do so.

Attempt to make eye contact during the interview. In a study of interviewee behavior, most candidates looked into the interviewer's eyes 50 percent of the time or less. Most of the time they made eye contact when they were being asked questions, and looked away as they began answering them. This is important, because if you were to try to make *constant* eye contact, you would be violating a norm, which may make some interviewers uncomfortable. The best rule is to act as if you were comfortably speaking to a friend, doing what feels natural and comfortable to you.

Do not use the interview as an opportunity to make personal statements or credos. Alan B. came to an interview with a large legal corporation in jeans so that he could say, "It's a person's performance that should count, not his appearance." The interviewer, whom he later contacted, said he was rejected because he believed that Alan would always have one cause or another which might not help the company's interest, or possible even harm it.

As you respond, it is essential to look comfortable rather than awkward or guilty. When necessary, take a few seconds for a thoughtful pause. During that time, take a deep breath or two. Respond on the exhale, making sure that you have a lot of breath so that you don't appear to mumble.

While humor is generally a plus, be careful not to use it insensitively. If you are asked a serious question and answer with a joke, you will not be looked on favorably. If there has to be a butt to your joke, avoid put-down humor, and use self-deprecating humor instead. Even with self-deprecating humor, do not use it to such excess that the interviewer will look at it as an indication of a lack of self-confidence. Use it to show that you do not take yourself too seriously.

Maintain total honestly. If you are not honest and get discovered, you will be disqualified. There is an old Slavic saying: Lies have very short legs. They cannot run very fast, and tend to trip over themselves. With this statement in mind, here is a direct contradiction. You must engage in a little puffery or exaggeration. Most interviewers expect you to exaggerate a bit, therefore they will deflate most things you say. If you are totally accurate, chances are you will end up being evaluated a bit south of your true ability. Most interviewers will subtract or deflate what you say by 10 to 20 percent to account for the Puffery Quotient.

Use the full palette of presentation tools to keep the interviewer's interest. In most cases, you will be one of many candidates for the position. Listening to a group of nervous candidates responding in monotone voices can be maddening. To help bring out your qualities, vary your voice during the presentation. You can do this by varying pitch. Too many speakers go up or down the equivalent of one note in their speech. They tend to sound robotic. A good speaker will go up or down a full octave. Listen to good radio and TV announcers and commentators. Forget the content, and follow their changes in pitch. Vary your volume too. You can draw people in by raising your voice when you are excited, or lowering your voice when you want to indicate the secretive or confidential nature of the information you are divulging. You can also speed up or slow down to communicate excitement or seriousness. Begin listening to good speakers as models.

Become sensitive to the interviewer. Years ago I studied a form of Kung Fu called Wing Chun. One of the major exercises we practiced for hours on end is called Sticky Hands. The key to this form of martial arts is guarding your centerline where all the good stuff is located (groin, stomach, face, and so on). The way the drill works is one partner places his or her hands on the other's. Both partners press their hands, equaling the pressure of the other. The notion is that if you move your hands too weakly, your opponent can push you out of the way and drive a blow to your center (for example, to your face, your throat, your solar plexus...or lower. Ouch). If you push too hard, your opponent can collapse, let you push your defense past your center, and leave you just as vulnerable as if you pushed weakly. The only way to protect yourself is to match your partner's force exactly.

Many Asian business people refer to Sun Tzu's book *The Art of War* as a major reference for conducting business. Being interviewed is hardly a war, but the idea of being sensitive to the tone, manner, and style of your interviewer, and *matching* these, is essential. Success begins with early preparation and constant vigilance.

Help the interview flow smoothly. If the interviewer seems nervous or inexperienced, help him or her out. If the interviewer is very domineering, don't compete. Remember that the interviewer controls the questions, but you control the content through your answers. The interviewer asks questions because he or she is interested in the answers. Make sure that you answer those questions directly. If you want to digress or expand on the question, ask permission to go outside of it.

Learn to deal with silence in the interview. Some interviewers use silence as a stress tool. If you give a response and it is greeted by silence, do not keep changing your view, or adding to it. This shows a lack of conviction on your part. You have two choices here. Let the interviewer break the silence with a comment or question, or ask a related question yourself.

Bring a pen and paper to the interview. Have these available to you in case the interviewer asks you to take down some information. Immediately after leaving write down all pertinent information you can remember, while it is still fresh in your mind. You can use it to review for future interviews in the company.

Practice Exercise 29: Preparing to Relax

Practice relaxation by visualizing yourself in the waiting room. Review Chapter 2 for techniques on calming your body and your mind. Your goal is to picture the clock, the setting, and yourself in interview attire *without* freezing up from nerves.

When you get to the actual interview situation, picture yourself at home relaxing. This is the time to get your muscles to relax, and your mind to become alert by oxygenating the brain. Do not smoke or chew gum during the interview, no matter how much it calms you. Do not drink alcohol to calm yourself. Even drinking the night before can influence your performance during the interview. Above all, *do* remember to breathe.

Practice Exercise 30: Practice Interviews

Carry out mock interviews. After you have done all the preparation, find a friend or two that can give you practice by asking you typical interview questions. The best way to practice is to simulate the interview situation as closely as possible. For example, it is somewhat helpful if a family member asks you these questions at the kitchen table and gives you a chance to practice your responses. It would be much better to find someone who is in the same field and knows the area. He or she can present you with intelligent follow-up questions that would closely simulate the actual interview situation, and critique your responses. Also, it is better to wear a suit or business dress, and take the mock interview in someone's office. All of these things will make you feel more comfortable during the actual interview. Cut down on as much of the novelty as you can.

After a few mock interviews, try to actually apply for some jobs that you do not really care about, just to get in some interview experience. You can also do this by going to job agencies and head hunters' offices where you will be interviewed.

Practice Exercise 31:
Rethinking Your Fear-Provoking Thoughts

Two sets of devastating thoughts can lead to anxiety: your negative predictions about your impending performance, and the importance of the consequences. Using the techniques in the earlier parts of this book (especially Chapters 3, 4, and 5), identify all the counter-evidence you can use to *refute* the idea that you will not be able to perform well under the pressure of the interview. Recall other job interviews in which you thought you did well. Write down specific examples of your ability to articulate your responses and to relate to interviewers.

Challenge any thoughts that this will be your only opportunity at a job like this. Identify the many "one-in-a-million" opportunities you have experienced to date. Your goal here is to label this opportunity as important rather than crucial. Remember, there is a difference between rare and once-in-a-lifetime.

If All Doesn't Go Well

Avoid personalizing the results of interviews (past and present) where you do not get the job. There are many reasons why you may interview well and not get selected for a job. For all you know, the interview may have been a formality, and the company may already know who they want to fill the position. In many cases, public companies and governmental offices have to do broad searches because of contract specifications, even though they just intend to hire people from the inside. They may have to hire the manager's brother-in-law. Once again, the more insecure and vulnerable someone is, the more he or she self-blames and personalizes rejection. It is essential to judge your *performance*, not your results.

By far the most important thing you can do in taking interviews is to identify your strengths. Plan a good way to present them where you sound confident, without sounding like you are bragging. Then focus your attention and energy during the interview on making sure these points get brought out. As you focus on the positive aspects of your presentation, you will look forward to the interview rather than dreading it.

Auditions

Auditions are like interviews for performers, with a few differences. First of all, in the area of preparation you know what you will have to do because you practice it all the time. There are still a few exceptions, of course. For example, symphonic musicians may be asked to sight read a piece of unfamiliar music, and actors may be asked to do a cold reading. For the most part, however, you are doing something for which you have been preparing, and which you like to do. You will have to take several potentially stressful factors into account when going on an audition. Each one presents a possible pitfall, but also an opportunity to master the solution. Both pitfalls and solutions are presented below.

Audition Pitfalls and Solutions

Pitfall: *Novelty*

With interviews, you generally know that you are going to end up in an office, sitting in a moderately comfortable chair. Auditions can end up being held in some very strange places. Susan X. was an opera singer who ended up having to do an audition for *Rigeletto* in a small room with a piano. Generally, operatic auditions are held in concert halls or theaters because the singers need to be able to project their voices without the aid of amplification. She was totally unnerved when she found herself in a small room having to try and project.

When auditioning, sometimes you may find yourself the only performer in the room. At other times you may be one of many people auditioning. In many cases a singer or instrumentalist may have to perform with an accompanist whom he or she would not have selected if given a choice. Actors may find themselves in a room with a casting director, producers, director, other actors, and so on. It is not uncommon to have people talking or offering other distractions while you are performing. There may also be distracting noises.

Solution:

You must be able to block all this distraction out by focusing on your performance. One good way to do this is implosion therapy. Practice under novel conditions of your own design, working your way up to a level of distraction that no audition could ever match. This will help you learn to maintain your attention, and will give you confidence beyond measure. You can do this by leaving the door open so that you can hear distracting sounds. Additional distractions while you practice can include not turning off the telephone ringer, having the radio on softly while you rehearse, or even asking people to stop in randomly to ask you something. Be creative, and then force yourself to maintain concentration.

Pitfall: *Dealing With the Competition*

If you are unfortunate enough to see, hear, or even smell your competition, you will find yourself saying that they are more attractive, more talented, can play faster, and even have better hair than you. Chances are you will emphasize *their strengths* and *your weaknesses.* Furthermore, you will notice that their strengths are always in the areas of your weaknesses and vulnerabilities.

Solution:

This is a time either to leave the room to be alone so you can ignore the competition, or to focus on your own strengths. Imagine what the competition finds intimidating about *you.*

Pitfall: *Attitudes Toward Performers*

In many cases, people coming to auditions are not treated very nicely. Instead of being treated like talented, well-trained artists, they are treated like livestock. There is rarely an ounce of empathy directed at you. You may find yourself treated rudely and insensitively. It is unfortunate, but this is what happens when supply exceeds demand.

Solution:
The only way to deal with such rudeness is by ignoring it, or developing great revenge fantasies. Just think how you'll treat these same "authorities" when you make it big.

Pitfall: *Formal Evaluations*

Many performers don't know which is worse: when the people doing the hiring are occasionally distracted, or when they stare and take notes on their clipboards.

Solution:
If you do not like to face evaluation, this is the wrong place to be. Again, you should practice in front of people who will give you notes or criticism, and do so harshly. This will prepare you for the situation so that you will not be dealing with it only during an audition.

Audition Preparation

As with the interview, the key to audition success is the right kind of preparation. Learn to practice your *vulnerable areas* rather than your strengths. Nobody likes to look or sound bad; consequently many people only practice their strengths. This keeps them feeling talented and secure ... until an audition. Then their weaknesses and vulnerabilities panic them.

The Case of Donald Y.

Donald Y. was a tenor who had a beautiful voice until he got to the top of his range. Then he started to sing like Alfalfa from the *Little Rascals*. His voice would sometimes reach B^b nicely, and sometimes it would crack. Singing a high C was like playing roulette, only the odds were safer for roulette. He practiced a great deal, but unfortunately he worked on his tone and musicality, which were already quite good. He avoided the dangerous high end of his register. This made him depressed, and who wants to feel depressed? Eventually,

Donald found a new teacher and got a new approach to the high end of his voice. Six months of constant practice later, Donald could sing a high C with confidence. He no longer panicked at auditions, worrying about what would happen when he got to the inevitable high notes.

Pitfall: *Over-Judging Your Performance*

Mimi A., an opera singer, never had an audition in which she thought she sang well. She won roles and was told she sounded good by people whom she respected, but that did not matter...she knew that she had not performed well. What happened to Mimi is very common with musicians and other performers. She was a very gifted and well-trained singer. As her training advanced, she stopped worrying about singing the correct notes. Her goals were loftier, and much more abstract. For example, Mimi would aim for a certain roundness of tone for certain passages. If she did not attain it, she would consider her performance a failure and found it difficult to deal with the fact that competent musicians and conductors would tell her they enjoyed her performance.

Solution:

What Mimi did not take into account was that the audience was not aware if her abstract goals. All they heard was beautiful singing. Mimi had reached a level which she never dipped under. She always gave a professional performance.

Because of a tendency to think in all-or-nothing terms, Mimi would rate her performances as either terrible or great: either a 0 or 100. In truth, using this scale, she would fluctuate more in a range from 87 to 99. She was actually always good—it was just a matter of how good.

How reasonable is your personal evaluation scale?

Pitfall: *Dealing With Uncertainty and Lack of Control*

Life would be good if the most talented people always got the awards, roles, and jobs. Alas, life and auditions are not like that. One of the most difficult things for people to deal with is the role of politics in the audition process. If you graduated from a certain university, studied with a certain teacher, or are affiliated with a certain agent, you might pass the audition. If you think this through, however, you can use uncertainty as a positive force. It does make rejections easier to deal with (considering that rejections are still always difficult to deal with under any circumstances).

The Solution:

The key to dealing with this high level of uncertainty is goal setting. Do not set yourself a goal of getting hired, or even getting called back. That is a goal that is not at all under your control. Set practice and performance goals. It is reasonable to set goals for how many hours a day you will practice, and what should be covered during those sessions. You can set goals for practicing coping strategies such as relaxation and stress inoculation. You can also set performance goals such as concentrating or making audience contact. If you meet your goals, you greatly increase the likelihood that the audition will be a success.

Pitfall: *Revealing Anxiety Symptoms*

Stuart P. was a manager at a high tech company. He came to me because he got extremely tense when speaking in public. His biggest concern was sweat. He would sweat profusely under his arms, leaving huge rings of perspiration. He would compound the problem by wearing extra layers of clothes to try to absorb the sweat. Needless to say the extra clothes made him hotter, and he sweated more.

Solution:

I suggested that Stuart go into his next talk and not try to hold the sweat back: just let it go. He was stunned. He imagined that letting it go would mean torrents of sweat. He got to understand that trying not to sweat took so much energy that it caused him to sweat more. When Stuart released himself from preventing the sweat, he relaxed and produced much less sweat. This technique is called *Paradoxical Intention*. As you feel anxiety symptoms, try to exaggerate them rather than trying to eliminate them. If you succeed, you may find it getting difficult to produce these symptoms.

Practice Exercise 32: Decreasing Surprise

As you use Paradoxical Intention, you will be doing another interesting thing. You will be looking more closely at your own anxiety. Each person manifests anxiety in a unique way, even though there are commonalties. Try the following exercise suggested by Eloise Ristad in her book *A Soprano on Her Head*.

As you rehearse, focus on trying to *intensify* anxiety symptoms you experience when you perform. At the same time, you will improve your ability to identify your particular symptoms of anxiety. This will decrease surprise when they occur. When you get up to perform, the surge of adrenaline that goes coursing through your body should seem like an old, familiar friend. By practicing while you are experiencing anxiety symptoms, you will get used to performing with them. If you find it difficult to produce the anxiety symptoms, try engaging in a physical activity that mirrors those symptoms, such as running in place or jumping rope. This will give you trembling hands and shortness of breath. From here, it will be easier to generate anxiety.

Practice Exercise 33: Relabeling Emotions

In a series of now-classic experiments, social psychologist Stanley Schacter got college students to experience the physical symptoms of anxiety and label them differently. He gave one set of students feedback that they were having the time of their lives, and another that they were having a really bad set of experiences. In many cases, he induced physiological symptoms with drugs such as epinephrine (adrenaline). As you might guess, the students who were told to expect good feelings *enjoyed* the rush of adrenaline, while those who dreaded the experience felt the adrenaline as negative anxiety.

Think about it. What do you feel like when you are exhilarated or ecstatic? Your heart pounds, you sweat, and your blood pressure rises. Does this sound at all familiar? The symptoms are the same as they are for anxiety! The difference is in what you call it. A musician sitting at home practicing alone will rarely have a transcendent experience performing a piece of music. Generally when you are practicing alone, your hormones take a nap. If a few friends happen to stop by, the hormones will awaken. You will begin to feel a sense of excitement. You cannot experience excitement without physical symptoms . . . so, why not learn to call them excitement rather than anxiety? Without the adrenaline wake-up call, a performance would be flat and lifeless. You need those symptoms to generate excitement. We have all witnessed athletic teams, artists, and other performers giving a flat performance. They got through their performance, but the energy was missing. What you experience as stagefright can be called excitement or anxiety. It's your choice.

Summary:

This chapter has presented survival skills for interviews and auditions. These include:

- Familiarizing yourself with various interview formats
- Preparing to answer questions about yourself, the company, and the industry
- Interview do's and don'ts
- Using relaxation techniques and mock interviews to prepare
- Anticipating common audition pitfalls
- Using such techniques as "Paradoxical Intention" and positive thinking to combat anxiety symptoms
- Relabeling your emotions to convert anxiety to positive energy

THE FINAL EVALUATION

Now that you have completed the book, turn the page and take the *D-M Stagefright Inventory* again. In this way you can see how much performance anxiety you currently have, compared to where you were when you began the book.

In a sense, controlling stagefright is an endless process because you will always come up against new situations, or reinterpret old ones. Fortunately, the same techniques you practiced here will work with new situations. You will also notice that as you practice the techniques in this book, it will become progressively easier to use them, freeing you to experience the pleasure of performing before others and letting them know who you really are!

D-M STAGEFRIGHT INVENTORY

Directions: Each item of this inventory is composed of a group of statements. Select the one that *best* describes the way you react when you perform before an audience. Circle the *number* beside the statement you select.

A

0 I do not try to avoid situations in which I must perform.
1 I occasionally try to avoid situations in which I must perform.
2 I usually try to avoid situations in which I must perform.
3 I always try to avoid situations in which I must perform.

B

0 I am not afraid that I will forget or blank out when performing.
1 I am sometimes afraid that I will forget or blank out on part of my performance.
2 I am afraid I will forget or blank out on large parts of my performance.
3 I am afraid that I will forget or blank out totally when performing.

C

0 I do not think others will be bored when I am performing.
1 I sometimes think others will be bored when I am performing.
2 I often think others will be bored when I am performing.
3 I always think others will be bored when I am performing.

D

0 When I perform, I do not experience difficulty in breathing.
1 When I perform, I sometimes experience difficulty in breathing.
2 When I perform, I often experience difficulty in breathing.
3 When I perform, I always experience difficulty in breathing.

E

0 I do not get nervous performing for an audience who is as competent or less competent than I.
1 I occasionally get nervous performing for an audience who is as competent or less competent than I.
2 I usually get nervous performing for an audience who is as competent or less competent than I.
3 I always get nervous performing for an audience who is as competent or less competent than I.

F

0 I do not think others will ridicule my performance.
1 I sometimes think others will ridicule my performance.
2 I often think others will ridicule my performance.
3 I always think others will ridicule my performance.

G

0 I am unaffected by the consequences of my performance.
1 I get nervous only when the consequences of my performance are very important.
2 I get nervous when the consequences of my performance are moderately important.
3 I get nervous regardless of the consequences.

H

0 I do not think that I will perform poorly.
1 I sometimes think that I will perform poorly.

2 I often think that I will perform poorly.

3 I always think that I will perform poorly.

I

0 I do not think that others will dislike me when I perform.

1 I sometimes think that others will dislike me when I perform.

2 I often think that others will dislike me when I perform.

3 I always think that others will dislike me when I perform.

J

0 I am not affected by the size of the audience.1 I only get nervous performing for a very large audience.

2 I get nervous performing for small audiences.

3 All audiences make me nervous.

K

0 I never have difficulty in concentrating when performing.

1 I sometimes have difficulty in concentrating when performing.

2 I often have difficulty in concentrating when performing.

3 I always have difficulty in concentrating when performing.

L

0 People do not feel sorry for me when they see me perform.

1 People sometimes feel sorry for me when they see me perform.

2 People often feel sorry for me when they see me perform.

3 People always feel sorry for me when they see me perform.

M

0 I do not feel nervous when performing for strangers.

1 I occasionally feel nervous when performing for strangers.

2 I usually feel nervous when performing for strangers.

3 I always feel nervous when performing for strangers.

N

0 The audience does not sense that I do not know my material.

1 The audience sometimes senses that I do not know my material.

2 The audience often senses that I do not know my material.

3 The audience always senses that I do not know my material.

O

0 I do not think that there is something about me that audiences dislike.

1 I occasionally think that there is something about me that audiences dislike.

2 I often think that there is something about me that audiences dislike.

3 I always think that there is something about me that audiences dislike.

P

0 I do not get embarrassed when performing.

1 I sometimes get embarrassed when performing.

2 I often get embarrassed when performing.

3 I always get embarrassed when performing.

Q

0 I am usually well organized when performing.

1 I sometimes appear disorganized when performing.

2 I often appear disorganized when performing.

3 I always appear disorganized when performing.

R

0 I do not expect to be put on the spot and attacked.

1 I sometimes expect to be put on the spot and attacked.

2 I often expect to be put on the spot and attacked.

3 I always expect to be put on the spot and attacked.

S

0 When performing in public, I do not experience trembling or shaking.

1 When performing in public, I sometimes experience trembling or shaking.

2 When performing in public, I often experience trembling or shaking.

3 When performing in public, I always experience trembling or shaking.

T

0 When I perform, I am usually well rehearsed.
1 When I perform, I sometimes do not rehearse enough.
2 When I perform, I often do not rehearse enough.
3 When I perform, I never rehearse enough.

U

0 If I perform well, the audience will not find anything wrong.
1 If I perform well, the audience occasionally still finds something wrong.
2 If I perform well, the audience often still finds something wrong.
3 If I perform well, the audience always finds something wrong.

V

0 I do not feel anxious once I have gotten started with my performance.
1 I feel somewhat anxious after I have gotten started with my performance.
2 I feel very anxious after I have gotten started with my performance.
3 I feel extremely anxious after I have gotten started with my performance.

W

0 I do not expect to make a lot of mistakes.
1 I sometimes expect to make a lot of mistakes.
2 I often expect to make a lot of mistakes.
3 I always expect to make a lot of mistakes.

X

0 I do not expect the audience to reject my point of view.
1 I sometimes expect the audience to reject my point of view.
2 I often expect the audience to reject my point of view.
3 I always expect the audience to reject my point of view.

Y

0 I do not feel nervous when performing for people who do not know me.

1 I sometimes feel nervous when performing for people who do not know me.

2 1 often feel nervous when performing for people who do not know me.

3 1 always feel nervous when performing for people who do not know me.

Scoring the Inventory

Add up the total number of points you have circled. Use the scale below to interpret your current level of stagefright on the inventory:

Above 40 .... Very High Stagefright

30-39 .... High Stagefright

20-29 .... Moderate Stagefright

0-19 .... Low Stagefright

0-9 .... Minimal Stagefright

References

Altmaier, E., M. Leary, S. Halpern, and J. Sellers. 1985. Effects of stress inoculation and participant modeling on confidence and anxiety. *Journal of Social and Clinical Psychology* 3(4): 500–505.

Beatty, M., and S. Payne. 1983. Speech anxiety as a multiplicative function of size of audience and social desirability. *Perceptual and Motor Skills* 56(2): 792–794.

Beck, A., and G. Emory. 1985. *Anxiety Disorders and Phobias: A Cognitive Perspective*. New York: Basic Books.

Benson, H. 1975. *The Relaxation Response*. New York: Morrow Books.

Booth, R., D. Bartlett, and J. Bohnsack. 1992. An examination of the relationship between happiness, loneliness, and shyness in college students. *Journal of College Student Development* 33(2): 157–162

Burns, D. 1980. *Feeling Good: The New Mood Therapy*. New York: New American Library.

Buss, A. 1980. *Self-Consciousness and Social Anxiety*. San Francisco: W.H. Freeman and Company.

Caspi, A., G.H. Elder, and D.J. Bem. 1989. Moving away from the world: Life-course patterns of shy children. *Annual Progress in Child Psychiatry and Child Development* 275–293.

Dawson, R. 1982. Comparing contributions of cognitive behavior therapy strategies in the treatment of speech anxiety. *Australian Journal of Psychology* 34(3): 277–308.

Desberg, P., G. Marsh, and C. Crandell. 1984. Dispositional correlates of audience anxiety. Paper presented at the Western Psychological Association Meetings, Los Angeles.

Ellis, A. 1962. *Reason and Emotion in Psychotherapy*. New York: Lyle Stuart Press.

Fredrick, G., and B. Goss 1984. Systematic desensitization in avoiding communication. In *Avoiding Communication: Shyness, Reticence, and Communication Apprehension*. J. Daly, and J. McCroskey (Eds.) Beverly Hills, California: Sage Publications.

Fremouw, W. 1984. Cognitive-behavioral therapies for modification of communication apprehension. In *Avoiding Communication: Shyness, Reticence, and Communication Apprehension*. J. Daly, and J. McCroskey (Eds.). Beverly Hills, California: Sage Publications.

Freud, S. 1905. *Jokes and Their Relation to the Unconscious*. New York: Norton Books.

Gross, R., and W. Fremouw. 1982. Cognitive restructuring and progressive relaxation for treatment of empirical subtypes of speech anxious subjects. *Cognitive-Therapy and Research* 6(4): 429–436.

Hayes, B., and W. Marshall. 1984. Generalization of treatment effects in training public speakers. *Behavior Research and Therapy* 22(5): 519–533.

Hekmat, H., R. Lubitz, and R. Deal. 1984. Semantic desensitization: A paradigmatic intervention approach to anxiety disorders. *Journal of Clinical Psychology* 40(2): 463–466.

Jackson, J., and B. Latane. 1981. All alone in front of all those people: Stage fright as a function of number and type of co-performers and audience. *Journal of Personality and Social Psychology* 40(1): 73–85.

Jaremko, M., R. Hadfield, and W. Walker. 1980. Contribution of an educational phase to stress inoculation of speech anxiety. *Perceptual Motor Skills* 50(2): 495–501.

Johnson, R.L., and C.R. Glass. 1989. Heterosocial anxiety and direction of attention in high school boys. *Cognitive Therapy and Research* 13(5): 509–526.

Kelly, L. 1984. Social skills training as a mode of treatment for social communications problems. In *Avoiding Communication: Shyness, Reticence, and Communication Apprehension.* J. Daly, and J. McCroskey (Eds.). Beverly Hills, California: Sage Publications.

Kirsch, I., M. Wolpin, and J. Knutson. 1975. A comparison of in-vivo methods for rapid reduction of "stage fright" in the college classroom: A field experiment. *Behavior Therapy* 6: 165–171.

Klatzky, R. 1980. *Human Memory: Structures and Processes.* San Francisco: W.H. Freeman.

Koudas, O. 1967. Reduction of examination anxiety and stage-fright by group desensitization and relaxation. *Behavioral Research and Therapy* 5: 275–281.

Leary, M. 1983. *Understanding Social Anxiety: Social, Personality and Clinical Perspectives.* Beverly Hills, California: Sage Publications.

Lent, R., R. Russell, and K. Zamostny. 1981. Comparison of cue controlled desensitization, rational restructuring and a credible placebo in the treatment of speech anxiety. *Journal of Consulting and Clinical Psychology* 49(4): 608–610.

Lucas, J., and H. Lorayne. 1985. *The Memory Book.* New York: Ballantine Books.

Marsh, G., P. Desberg, and C. Crandall. 1983. Effects of social anxiety on memory for names. Paper presented at the Western Psychological Association meeting, San Francisco.

Marshall, W., L. Parker, and B. Hayes. 1982. Treating public speakers problems: A study using flooding and elements of skills training. *Behavior Modification* 6(2): 147–170.

McCrosky, J. 1977. Oral communication apprehension: A summary of recent theory and research. *Human Communication Research* 4: 78–96.

McKinney, M., and R. Gatchel. 1982. Comparative effectiveness of heart rate, biofeedback, speech skills training and a combination of both in treating public speaking anxiety. *Biofeedback and Self-Regulation* 7(1): 71–87.

McKinney, M., R. Gatchel, and P. Paulus. 1983. The effects of audience size on high and low speech anxious subjects during an actual speaking task. *Basic and Applied Social Psychology* 4(1): 73–87.

Melchior, L.A., and J.M. Cheek. 1990. Shyness and anxious self-preoccupation during a social interaction. *Journal of Social Behavior and Personality 5(2): 117–130*

Montgomery, R.L., F. Haemmerlie, and M. Edwards. 1991. Social, personal, and interpersonal deficits in socially anxious people. *Journal of Social Behavior and Personality* 6(4): 859–872.

Norton, G., L. MacLean, and E. Wachna. 1978. The use of cognitive desensitization and self directed mastery training for treating stage fright. *Cognitive Therapy and Research* 2(1): 61–64.

Olivier, L. 1982. *Confessions of an Actor: An Autobiography.* New York: Simon and Schuster.

Osberg, J. 1981. The effectiveness of applied relaxation in the treatment of speech anxiety. *Behavior Therapy* 12(5): 723–729.

Rickman, M.D., and R.J. Davidson. 1994. Personality and Behavior in Parents of Temperamentally Inhibited and Uninhibited Children. *Developmental Psychology* 30, n3: 346–354.

Ristad, E. 1982. *A Soprano on Her Head.* Moab, Utah: Real People Press.

Smith, J. 1975. *Relaxation Dynamics: Nine World Approaches to Self-Relaxation.* Champaign, Illinois: Research Press.

Smith, M. 1975. *When I Say No I Feel Guilty.* New York: Dial Press.

Wallace, A., D. Wallechinsky, and I. Wallace. 1983. *The Book of Lists.* New York: Morrow, Books.

Watson, D., and R. Tharp. 1977. *Self-Directed Behavior: Self-Modification for Personal Adjustment.* Monterey, California: Brooks-Cole.

Weissberg, M. 1977. A comparison of direct and vicarious treatments of speech anxiety: Desensitization, desensitization with coping imagery and cognitive modification. *Behavior Therapy* 8: 606–620.

Worthington, E.C. 1984. Speech and coping skills training and paradox as treatment for college students anxious about public speaking. *Perceptual Motor Skills* 59(2): 3394.

Woy, J., and J. Efran. 1972. Systematic desensitization and expectancy in the treatment of speaking anxiety. *Behavioral Research and Therapy* 10: 43–49.

Zettle, R.D., and S. Hayes. 1983. The Effects of social context on the impact of coping self-statements. *Psychological Reports* 52(2): 391–401.

Zimbardo, P. 1977. *Shyness: What it is What to do About it.* Reading: Addison-Wesley Publishing Company.

Suggested Readings

Aaron, S. 1986. *Stage Fright: Its Role in Acting.* Chicago: Chicago University Press.

Caldwell, R. 1990. *The Performer Prepares.* Dallas: PST . . . Inc.

Havas, K. 1973. *Stage Fright: Its Causes and Cures with Special References to Violin Playing.* London: Bosworth & Co.

Humes, J.C. 1975. *Podium Humor.* New York: Harper and Row

Markway, B.G., C.N. Carmin, C.A. Pollard, and T. Flynn. 1992. *Dying of Embarrassment: Help for Social Anxiety & Phobia.* Oakland. California: New Harbinger Publications, Inc.

Marshall, J.R. 1994. *Social Phobia: From Shyness to Stage Fright.* New York: Basic Books.

Medley, H.A. 1984. *Sweaty Palms: The Neglected Art of Being Interviewed.* Berkeley, California: Ten Speed Press.

Ross, J. 1994. *Triumph Over Fear.* New York: Bantam Books.

Snyder, M. 1987. *Public Appearances/Private Realities: The Psychology of Self-Monitoring.* New York: W.H. Freeman and Company.

Yate, M.J. 1995. *Knock 'em Dead: With Great Answers to Tough Interview Questions.* Boston: Bob Adams, Inc.

Other New Harbinger Self-Help Titles